Birnbaum's

Walt Disney World®

for KID$ by kids

Tom Passavant
EDITORIAL DIRECTOR

Cynthia Ambrose
ART DIRECTOR

Deanna Caron
Elisa Gallaro
SENIOR EDITORS

Mark F. Spoonauer
CONTRIBUTING EDITOR

Alexandra Mayes Birnbaum
CONSULTING EDITOR

HYPERION AND HEARST BUSINESS PUBLISHING, INC.

ISBN: 0-7868-8112-7

Printed in the United States of America

An enormous debt of gratitude is owed to Diane Hancock, Robert Sias, Bob Mervine, Wendy Wolfe, Michael Mendenhall, Laura Simpson, Kelly Slagle, Mickey Metz, Gene Duncan, Amy Sadowsky, Kevin Meyers, Marc Glissman, Jack Blitch, all of whom performed above and beyond the call of duty to make the creation of this book possible. To Phil Lengyel, Tom Elrod, Linda Warren, Bob Miller, and Charlie Ridgway, thank you for believing in this project in the first place. And to Wendy Lefkon, special thanks for taking it from idea to reality.

Other 1996 Birnbaum Travel Guides

Bahamas, and Turks & Caicos
Bermuda
Canada
Cancun/Cozumel & Isla Mujeres
Caribbean
Country Inns & Back Roads
Disneyland
Hawaii
Mexico
Miami & Fort Lauderdale
United States
Walt Disney World
Walt Disney World Without Kids

CONTENTS

We Wrote This Book!

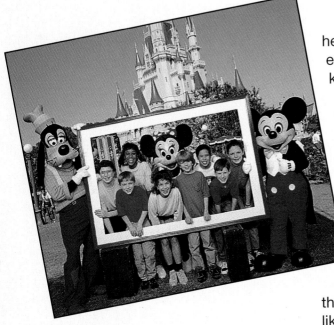

here's a guide written especially for kids, by the kids you see in the photos. To create this book, they traveled to Walt Disney World with us, the editors of *Birnbaum's Walt Disney World*. We took kids ages 8 to 14 to get opinions from each age group. We went on several trips with different groups of kids each time and did our best to see all the things we thought you would like the most. We also stood

Yes! You're going to Walt Disney World, home of Mickey Mouse, Space Mountain, Tower of Terror, and much more. But once you get there, where should you start? What should you see first? And where should you and your family stay?

That's why we wrote this book—to answer your questions and help you plan the most awesome vacation in the World. We thought you would like a kids' perspective. So in line for everything so that we could tell you which attractions are worth the wait and which you should save for another time.

Since you won't have time to do it all, read the descriptions of the attractions and decide which ones you most want to see—and which you could live without. To the right and on the next few pages, we tell you a little bit about each of the kids who have participated in this project. The information about the kids will give you an idea of whose opinions might be most like your own.

Tate says, "I hope kids who read this book will appreciate my opinions and use them to make their trip as fun and exciting as possible."

We went on the most popular attractions twice, with different groups of kids to get a variety of opinions. The kids didn't always agree about each attraction. Even those who were the same age sometimes disagreed.

Justin Berfield

Justin, who lives in Oak Park, California, was 8 years old when he worked on this book. He's an actor, and has appeared in commercials, movies, and a television show. He loves animals and has some unusual pets.

Lindsay Compton

Lindsay, who lives in Dallas, Texas, was 9 years old when she worked on this book. She is a Girl Scout and also likes to play soccer and basketball. She loves to draw and plans to become an animal doctor when she grows up.

Bradley Sanchez

Bradley, who lives in Independence, Missouri, was 10 years old when he worked on this book. He likes to play football and is a fan of the Kansas City Chiefs. He enjoys playing video games.

Dawna Boone

Dawna, who lives in Natick, Massachusetts, was 11 years old when she worked on this book. She loves reading and listening to music. She also plays the alto and tenor saxophone in her school band and takes ballet classes.

Danielle Gould

Danielle, who lives in Potomac, Maryland, was 11 years old when she worked on this book. She enjoys reading and loves to dance. She takes ballet, jazz, and tap lessons.

Tate Lynche

Tate was 13 years old when he worked on this book, and was a Mouseketeer on "The Mickey Mouse Club" show. He lives in St. Petersburg, Florida. He wants to be an entertainer, but is also interested in directing and producing. He enjoys in-line skating.

Anna Kerlek

Anna, who lives in Chagrin Falls, Ohio, was 13 years old when she worked on this book. She plays on her school volleyball, basketball, and track teams, and she loves to sing and play the piano. She was a grand prize winner of the Delta World Adventure Essay Contest.

Adam Winchester

Adam, who was 14 years old when he worked on this book, lives in Colorado Springs, Colorado. His favorite sports are hockey, basketball, baseball, and soccer. He hopes to become an architect or to work with computers.

You may not always agree with the kids either. Even so, their ideas should help you decide how best to plan your trip.

During our visits, we spent many days touring the Magic Kingdom, Epcot, and the Disney-MGM Studios. We visited Discovery Island, ate in a wide variety of restaurants, and stopped by many of the hotels on the Disney grounds. We even had a chance to participate in an educational program.

To check out the newest attractions, we took some of the kids back for another visit. We got to ride Tower of Terror in the Disney-MGM Studios. At the Magic Kingdom, we explored the new and improved Tomorrowland. Another highlight was seeing the Legend of The Lion King, a new show in Fantasyland. Even Epcot has a brand-new attraction called Innoventions. It's a huge place with tons of hands-on activities, and the kids loved it. We also ate in new restaurants, including Planet Hollywood, the kids' favorite. A special treat was the new Wilderness Lodge Resort, where the kids enjoyed eating in the Whispering Canyon Café.

All the kids who have worked on this guide agree that a week-long stay isn't enough. If you really want to see all that Walt Disney World has to offer, the kids suggest you plan on spending 1½ to 2 weeks.

Altogether, we've spent almost 20 days and covered most of Walt Disney World, but we still have more to see. Walt Disney World is always changing and new things are added each year. So don't try to do everything in one trip. We'll be going back again to see what we missed, too. Only next time we'll take different kids to see the newest attractions and all the old favorites, so you'll have even more opinions to consider.

The book is organized into five chapters. The first

Robert Raack

Robert, who lives in Eugene, Oregon, was 8 years old when he worked on this book. He is very interested in dragons, and likes to play video games and soccer.

Taran Noah Smith

Taran was 9 years old when he worked on this book. He plays Mark Taylor, the youngest son on the hit show "Home Improvement." When he's not on the set, he lives in San Rafael, California. He likes to sail and ride his mountain bike.

Elisabeth Woodhams

Lissy, who lives in Tucson, Arizona, was 11 years old when she worked on this book. She plays the piano, is a member of her drama club, and enjoys horseback riding and swimming.

Ashley Pletz

Ashley, who lives in Chicago, Illinois, was 11 years old when she worked on this book. She loves to write. She also takes ballet lessons and has done some modeling.

Brian Levinthal

Brian, who lives in Huntington, New York, was 12 years old when he worked on this book. He is studying cartoon art, and plays the clarinet in the school band. He also likes to swim.

Karyn Williams

Karyn, who lives in Orlando, Florida, was 13 years old when she worked on this book. She is an aspiring actress. She also loves to travel, and once spent several weeks studying marine biology in Australia.

David Bickel

David, who lives in Columbus, Ohio, was 13 years old when he worked on this book. He is a major sports fan and enjoys playing baseball and video games. His favorite teams are the Atlanta Braves and the Chicago Bulls.

Thomanita Booth

Nita, who lives in Chesapeake, Virginia, was 14 years old when she worked on this book. She was a Mouseketeer on the "Mickey Mouse Club" show, and a member of the music group MMC. Nita also enjoys singing in her church choir.

three cover the theme parks. We describe each attraction, and then the kids offer their opinions. The fourth chapter covers places like Discovery Island, the hotels, restaurants, and other activities and attractions not in the parks. The last chapter is filled with hot tips from the kids on how to make your vacation even better.

Lots of things make this book interactive. There are places to put your own photos. The last page is ready for autographs. There also is space to make your lists of the attractions you most want to see and a section where you can plan your schedule.

We can't wait to hear what you think about this guide. So please write to us with your tips for the best vacation in the World at:
Walt Disney World
For Kids, By Kids;
1790 Broadway,
6th Floor;
New York, NY 10019.

Have a great trip!

The Magic Kingdom

The Magic Kingdom is probably the most special part of Walt Disney World. The soaring towers of Cinderella Castle, the odd-shaped white peak of Space Mountain, the carousel, the spinning teacups, and even the Dumbos flying through the air are the images that first come to mind when Walt Disney World is mentioned.

We spent lots of time exploring the seven "lands"—Main Street, Adventureland, Frontierland, Liberty Square, Fantasyland, Mickey's Starland, and Tomorrowland. The Magic Kingdom is packed with attractions, so it's important to plan ahead and set the order in which you'll visit them. This chapter can help you decide which attractions you most want to see. Then make a list of the attractions that fall into your "second choice" category and a list of the things you can live without. That way you can organize your visit and avoid wasting a lot of time.

While you're in the Magic Kingdom, notice the little details that make the place so special. The theme of the lands is shown in the costumes worn by the people who work there, the design of the shops and restaurants, and even the design of the trash bins.

MAIN STREET, U.S.A.

This is the Disney version of how a small-town Main Street would have looked around the year 1900. And it's perfect down to the last detail. There are hitching posts where townspeople would have tied up their horses and many other touches that make this Main Street so attractive. Crews of painters keep the buildings looking fresh. They work their way up one side of the street and back down the other. Then they start all over again. There aren't any major attractions on Main Street, but the Walt Disney World Railroad begins its journey here. There also are a few other interesting things to see.

Walt Disney World Railroad

Walt Disney was a big train buff. He even built a model railroad in his backyard! The trains that run on the Walt Disney World Railroad are real locomotives that were originally built around 1900. Disney Imagineers found them in Mexico in 1969. The trains have been completely overhauled, and all their parts have been replaced.

A ride on the railroad gives a quick overview of the Magic Kingdom. The full round trip takes about 20 minutes, but you can get on and off at any of the stations. Main Street is the starting point and ending point. In between, trains make stops in Frontierland and Mickey's Starland.

> **"It gets you to different lands much faster than walking."**
>
> —David (age 13)

Shopping

Main Street U.S.A. is lined with many different types of shops. There are places to buy candy, clothing, souvenirs, hats, cameras, jewelry, and books. Shops stay open a half-hour after the park closes to give you a little extra time. Shopping hints are on page 146 in the Everything Else in the World chapter.

The kids agree that the train is a nice way to travel around the park. "It's a great way to get around without walking, and the sights are nice, too," says Karyn. David agrees. "It gets you to different lands much faster than walking."

Main Street Cinema

Ever wonder how Mickey Mouse became a star? You'll find the answer in *Mickey's Big Break*, the short film shown in this theater. You'll also get to see Mickey in some of his early roles in classic cartoons. There are no seats, so don't stop here if you're tired.

"There's a big difference between the movies Disney used to put out and the ones they do now," says Dawna. Tate thinks "it's nice to see Mickey's beginnings."

The kids agree that the cinema is a bit boring. Anna's advice sums it up: "If you're pressed for time, don't make it one of your stops."

ADVENTURELAND

Adventureland combines the exotic islands of the Caribbean, Polynesia, and Southeast Asia. The landscaping features many plants and trees native to these islands. The buildings look like ones you might see if you traveled there. Adventureland has four main attractions—Pirates of the Caribbean, the Jungle Cruise, the Swiss Family Treehouse, and the Tropical Serenade.

Pirates of the Caribbean

See a pirate raid on a Caribbean island town as you float through this adventure. Cannons fire into the air while pirates attack and pillage a village. The song "Yo-Ho, Yo-Ho, A Pirate's Life For Me" is the ride's catchy theme. As you make your way through the different scenes, pay attention to details like the exploding flowerpots and the interesting faces of each pirate. Near the end, don't miss the pirate with his leg dangling over the bridge— the leg is actually hairy. There's one small flume drop during the ride, so be prepared.

"This is an excellent ride," says David. "My favorite part is the pirate ship with the wind blowing and all the cannons firing. And I love how the characters look real."

Karyn thinks the details are great, too. "I was really paying attention to things like the hair on that guy's leg, the pirate chasing the lady, and the fire—it all just looks so real," she says. Ashley notices the characters, also. "The costumes are neat," she says.

But Lissy thinks the ride is a little dull. "It's really slow and I'm not that into pirates, so it doesn't amuse me too much." Brian agrees. "It isn't as exciting as I

"It all just looks so real."
—Karyn (age 13)

thought the pirate was pointing his gun right at me—that's cool. The only part I'm not crazy about is the skull and crossbones. It's too dark."

"My favorite part is the pirate ship with the wind blowing and all the cannons firing."
—David (age 13)

thought it would be," he says. "I do like all the details and the way things look very realistic—especially the pirate's hairy leg."

Nita's favorite part is the dip. "There should be more dips, but it's still a cool ride," she says.

Robert agrees. "My favorite part has to be the drop," he says. "I

Jungle Cruise

Become an explorer on this journey through four far-away lands—a Southeast Asian jungle, the Nile valley, the African grasslands, and the Amazon rain forest. Along the way you'll see elephants, zebras, giraffes, lions, hippos, and even headhunters. The captain of the ship tells lots of corny jokes, so how much you enjoy the ride will depend on your guide. This ride is usually very crowded. Ask if the wait is more than 15 minutes. If it is, come back at another time.

Some of the kids think the ride is a little dull. "There isn't enough action in it," says David. "It would be neat if you got wet."

Nita agrees. "I think it's boring and not a good ride for teenagers," she says. "I'd recommend it if you have nothing better to do on a hot day."

Karyn thinks the Jungle Cruise is a "nice family ride. But the guide has a lot to do with how much you like it, and our guide wasn't very good." Ashley agrees. "I did not like our guide. His jokes were really stupid," she says.

Lissy and Robert like the Jungle Cruise. "The driver let me drive the boat for a while and that was really fun," says Lissy. "I like the way all the fake animals look real."

Robert agrees. "I love the ride," he says. "It would be even cooler if the headhunters really threw their spears."

Don't wait more than 15 minutes for this ride.

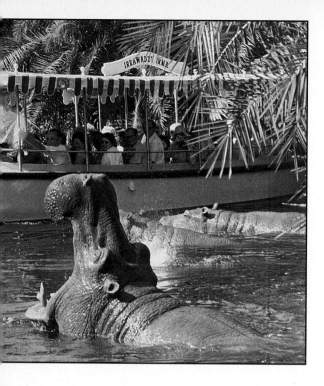

Swiss Family Treehouse

Before you go see the treehouse, it's a good idea to know something about the classic story of the Swiss Family Robinson. The Robinsons were traveling to New Guinea when their ship was wrecked on an island during a storm. Mr. Robinson and two of his three sons built a treehouse. Although the family was given several chances to leave the island, all but one son decided to stay. The treehouse was so comfortable that the family had "everything we need right at our fingertips," said Mr. Robinson.

Disney's version of the treehouse has many levels that you climb by way of a staircase. There are patchwork quilts on the beds, and there's running water in every room.

The tree is a creation of the Walt Disney World props department. It has 300,000 plastic leaves. Its concrete roots are set 42 feet into the ground.

Everyone agrees that reading the story or seeing the Disney movie about the Swiss Family Robinson makes the treehouse much more fun to explore.

"You have to know the story to

Try to read the book or see the movie about the Swiss Family Robinson before you visit this attraction.

understand it," says Karyn. "It's so neat after you know what you're looking at. My favorite room is the kitchen," she adds.

"Once you know the story, then the treehouse is fascinating," says David. "I like the boys' room with the hammocks and the running water."

Lissy agrees. "You wouldn't know why they built the treehouse in the first place. They did a good job of disguising it because it looks like a real tree."

Ashley likes the treehouse and says "the kitchen is my favorite."

Robert has seen the movie and read the book, so he really understood what he was seeing. "I could name all the rooms as we walked around," he says. "It's an excellent treehouse."

> **" Once you know the story, then the treehouse is fascinating. "**
>
> —David (age 13)

Tropical Serenade

Here's your chance to see the very first Walt Disney World attraction with Audio-Animatronics figures. Your hosts are José, Michael, Pierre, and Fritz. They introduce you to more than 200 birds, flowers, and tiki statues that sing and whistle a variety of songs.

The kids agree that this attraction is a little silly and outdated. But they do think it's interesting to see the early Audio-Animatronics figures and compare them with the newer ones.

"It's just a bunch of singing birds," says Lindsay. Brad thinks the songs go "too fast. It's hard to understand what they're saying."

For Dawna, "It doesn't matter how old you are, you will find this very boring. And it's too long."

Danielle and Anna, however, found things to like here. "The scenery is really pretty," says Danielle. Anna adds, "It's cool how the birds, flowers, and figures move their beaks and bodies with the words."

> "It doesn't matter how old you are, you will find this very boring."
> —Dawna (age 11)

FRONTIERLAND

Frontierland represents the American Frontier—from New England to the Southwest—from the 1770s to the 1880s. It includes two of the most popular attractions in the park. Both are mountains. You can take a watery trip down Splash Mountain and ride a runaway train at Big Thunder Mountain Railroad. Other attractions in Frontierland include the Country Bear Jamboree, the Diamond Horseshoe Saloon Revue, the Frontierland Shootin' Arcade, and Tom Sawyer Island.

Splash Mountain

This is the newest peak in the Magic Kingdom mountain range. You must be at least 44 inches tall to ride. At Splash Mountain, you travel in a log boat through brightly painted scenes from Walt Disney's movie, *Song of the South*. You'll see Brer Rabbit, Brer Fox, and Brer Bear getting into all kinds of trouble. There are three smaller dips during the ride, all leading up to the big drop—a sharp plunge down 52 feet going 40 miles per hour. If you're sitting in the front of the log, you get very wet. If you're in the back, you just get a small splash.

"It's really cool," says Taran. "The last drop is awesome!" Ashley agrees. "I like all the dips,

HOT TIP:

Sit in the front of the log if you want to get wet.

> ❝ **The last drop is awesome!** ❞
>
> —Taran (age 9)

> ❝ **When you're in the front, you get all drenched.** ❞
>
> —Brad (age 10)

but the last one is great. I like how my belly would flip-flop on the way down."

Brad loves getting wet. "When you're in the front, you get all drenched," he says. Lissy didn't get as wet. "The big drop is awesome, but you don't get too wet if you're sitting in the back of the log."

The kids agree that you have to go on the ride a few times before you can appreciate the scenery

and the story about Brer Rabbit, Brer Bear, and Brer Fox. "The dips are incredible," says Brian. "But I didn't know what was going on inside the mountain." Lissy agrees. "I didn't know the story until I heard the song 'Zip-A-Dee-Doo-Dah.' Then I knew where it was from."

Some of the kids were able to catch some of the details of the story. Lindsay says, "As it goes slow, you can see all the scenery. Every time there's a little splash, something different happens to Brer Rabbit." Brad agrees. "I love that story. Brer Rabbit is supposed to be in the log getting away from the fox and the bear."

Robert thinks "the scenery is really good, especially at the end when Brer Fox gets his tail pulled by an alligator." Tate says, "You really need to look at the story. It makes the ride even better."

Karyn agrees. "All the characters are so cute and so detailed, and of course, the last drop is great."

"The bears are great, and some of them are very funny."

—Brian (age 12)

Country Bear Jamboree

At this unusual country-and-western show, about 20 life-size Audio-Animatronics bears sing songs, play musical instruments, and tell a few jokes. It's a silly show, so it's important to go in with a silly attitude. Big Al,

"Two thumbs down and a couple of toes."

—Karyn (age 13)

one of the most popular bears, can't even carry a tune.

The show gets mixed reviews from the kids, with most of them not enthusiastic.

"It's strictly for little kids ages 2 to 6," says Lissy. "It's a serious waste of time for older kids."

Karyn agrees, giving the show a rating of "two thumbs down and a couple of toes. But I think little kids will like to sing along with the characters," she adds.

"The show is very boring," says David. "I hate country music, so I really don't like this show."

Still, some of the kids find something to like. For example, Ashley says she hates the show, "but the little bear that is unhappy and squeaks is kind of cute."

Brian thinks, "The bears are great, and some of them are very funny. The one that seems to be drunk and can't sing is really funny. I think the show is very enjoyable."

Big Thunder Mountain Railroad

Ride a roller coaster that races inside and outside Big Thunder Mountain. There are enough swoops and turns to keep this trip thrilling, but it's tamer than Space Mountain. You must be at least 40 inches tall to ride.

The runaway mine trains pass through several scenes with some real-looking chickens, donkeys, possums, and goats. This is a ride you can go on again and again, and still find new things to see each time. It's also a good ride to try once during the day and once at night. In the daytime, try to catch all the details of the flooded mining town. Look for the rainmaker and the man dressed in long johns as he spins through the flood in a bathtub. See if you can spot the party going on upstairs in the saloon.

The kids have only good things

"**I would ride it again and again.**"

—Danielle (age 11)

to say about this ride. "It's full of twists and turns," says Tate. Justin agrees. "I like all the turns. It's not too scary, but I was screaming because it's so much fun."

Adam says, "I love how there's a mining town down below. Don't miss the donkey wagging its tail." Lindsay also notices that "the background stuff is set up really nice. And I like that you feel like the ride is over, but then you go down another hill."

Anna thinks it's a great ride. "There are no huge drops, and it goes just fast enough to get a thrill. The scenery is great, too."

Danielle calls it "tame but really, really fun. I would ride it again and again."

PASTE
A
MAGIC
KINGDOM
PHOTO
HERE

Tom Sawyer Island

To reach Tom Sawyer Island, you take a raft ride across the Rivers of America. The island has hills to climb, a working windmill,

Read *The Adventures of Tom Sawyer* before visiting this island.

and two neat bridges. One is a swing bridge and the other is a barrel bridge. When one person bounces, everybody does. Across the bridges is Fort Sam Clemens, where there's a guardhouse with a bunch of Audio-Animatronics animals. The second floor of the fort has air guns that you can shoot.

"I kept jumping on the bridges," says Justin. "I also like the cave and the fort where you get to shoot out." Brad also had fun with the rifles. "I like pretending that I'm shooting something. I like the raft ride over, too."

Dawna recommends reading *The Adventures of Tom Sawyer* before visiting the island. "I think you have to read the book to understand the whole story. I like the raft ride over to the island because in the book, Tom takes a raft," she says.

Some of the older kids think the island is a little boring. "The bridges and caves are fun, but the rest is boring," says Adam. Tate agrees. "I thought it would be a big play place for kids since Tom Sawyer is a kid like us, but I don't think it's very special."

At the **Frontierland Shootin' Arcade**, you can fire rifles that send infrared beams at targets. Hit the tombstones and they rise, sink, and spin. Hit the gravedigger's shovel, and a skull pops out of the grave. (You have to pay extra to use the arcade. It's not included in your park admission.)

An energetic crew of singers and dancers perform all day at the **Diamond Horseshoe Saloon Revue**. The jokes are very corny, but the performers are entertaining.

LIBERTY SQUARE

Liberty Square is actually a small area that separates Frontierland from Fantasyland. It's a quiet spot with several shops and a couple of the Magic Kingdom's most popular attractions—the Haunted Mansion and The Hall of Presidents. There is one more Liberty Square attraction to see—the Liberty Square Riverboat.

Haunted Mansion

There are so many special effects inside the Haunted Mansion that you can go through it over and over again, and still not catch them all. It's not too scary, but there are enough surprises to keep you on your toes. When you enter the building, you're led into a hall where the host gives you an idea of what you're in for. The

"It's awesome! You never know what's going to come next."
—Lissy (age 11)

ceiling starts to rise and the walls begin to stretch—or at least that's how it seems. You're actually in an elevator that helps create these special effects. There's a moment before you board your "Doom Buggy" when the room is completely dark. It only lasts about 15 seconds, but for kids who are afraid of the dark, that's much too long.

Once on board your buggy, there are so many things to see. Try to watch for the raven that appears over and over again, the door knockers that knock themselves, the ghostly teapot pouring tea, and the dancing ghosts.

"It's awesome!" says Lissy. "It's kind of scary because you never know what's going to come next, so it's very surprising."

Dawna agrees. "I like how they have things popping out at you. And the dancing ghosts look so real." Danielle adds, "The special effects are great."

David thinks younger kids would be frightened by the ride. "I would recommend it for older kids who understand there's no such thing as ghosts," he says. Justin likes the Haunted Mansion but warns, "If you get scared easily, don't go."

Robert thinks that's good advice. "It's fun at the start, but then it gets pitch black and it's too scary," he says. "If you don't like the dark, this is not a ride for you."

But Lindsay still enjoyed the ride. "The man at the beginning tried to make it sound scary," she says. "When you actually go on the ride, it's not too spooky."

> " If you don't like the dark, this is not a ride for you. "
> —Robert (age 8)

The Hall of Presidents

The first part of this attraction is an interesting film that discusses the importance of the Constitution from the time it was written through the beginning of the Space Age. The famous poet, Maya Angelou, is the narrator.

Then the screen rises and all of the presidents, from George Washington to Bill Clinton, are represented by Audio-Animatronics figures. The Abraham Lincoln and Bill Clinton figures make speeches. Be sure to watch all the presidents closely because they move around, whisper to the person next to them, and shake hands.

The kids were pleasantly surprised by this attraction. Danielle says, "I thought it would be boring, but it isn't. It's very interesting." Lindsay agrees. "It's a fun way to learn," she says.

Brad thinks "it's like being on a school field trip. The Audio-Animatronics presidents look real, even though they're fake." Adam agrees. "The way they move makes it very realistic. I especially like Bill Clinton and Abraham Lincoln."

Justin likes that "it teaches about the presidents. A lot of the names I had never heard before." Dawna points out that "people usually know about George Washington and Abraham Lincoln and the current president, but not anyone in between." She also likes all the costumes.

The kids agree that when each president's name is announced, the spotlight on him should be brighter. Then it would be easier to find each president on stage.

"The way they move makes it very realistic."
—Adam (age 14)

Rivers of America

The **Liberty Square Riverboat**, named *Richard F. Irvine* after a Disney designer, is a real steamboat. The ride is slow, but it's a nice break on a hot afternoon. The best seats are right up front or in the back, where you can see both sides of the Rivers of America as you go along.

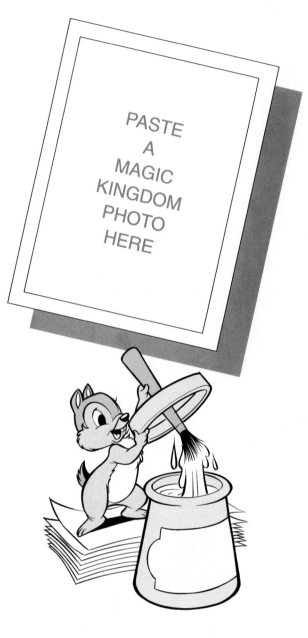

PASTE
A
MAGIC
KINGDOM
PHOTO
HERE

MICKEY'S STARLAND

Even though this area is known as Mickey's Starland, the town itself is called Duckburg, U.S.A. Inside one of the large tents is the Mickey's Starland Show. The other big tent is the Mickey Mouse Club Funland, where an interactive video display lets you see yourself on a screen. There also are lots of hands-on activities. You'll find Mickey's house in Duckburg. Be sure to go in and notice some of the details there. Mickey's radio plays Disney songs; there are photos of Walt Disney and Mickey Mouse on the walls; and the television set shows previews from The Disney Channel.

Along the business street in Duckburg, you'll see the Popcorn Shop where boxes out front pop when they're opened. At the firehouse, there's a working siren and a rotating light. On the sidewalk, you'll see stars with the names of Disney characters in them. When you step on the star, you'll hear the character's voice.

At Grandma Duck's Farm, you can get up close to some baby

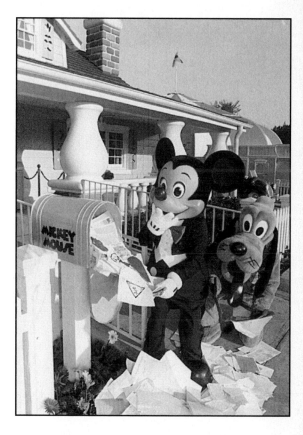

animals. You can also see Minnie Moo, a cow with natural markings that look just like Mickey Mouse ears. Near the farm is the Mouse-Ka-Maze, where trees and shrubs shaped like animals create a simple path for kids.

Mickey's Starland Show

This stage show stars Mickey Mouse and characters from the Disney Afternoon cartoons "Goof Troop," "Tale Spin," "Bonkers," and "Dark Wing Duck." Inside the pre-show area, you can watch clips from those cartoons and keep an eye on the countdown to showtime.

The show features a hostess who starts by singing a few songs with Mickey Mouse. Then she introduces the guest characters, like Goofy and his son Max, Bonkers, Baloo, Louie, and Dark Wing Duck. All the characters sing songs and act out skits, and the audience can sing along.

After the show, head for Mickey's dressing room, where

"I love the songs they sing and how you can get up and dance."

—Nita (age 14)

you can get his autograph and have your photo taken with him.

The show gets mixed reviews from the kids.

"I just didn't like it," says Taran. "It's good for younger kids, but not for kids like 8 to 10."

Nita feels differently. "I love it," she says. "I love the songs they sing and how you can get up and dance." She thinks there's a middle age where kids don't appreciate the show, but then "when you get to be around my age, you like it again." She agrees that it's great for little kids, too.

Like Nita, Karyn loves the show, "but I think there's a certain age when you don't appreciate it."

Brian likes the show but says, "If I were a little younger, I would have liked it more. I like watching the younger kids have fun," he adds.

David agrees. "Just seeing all the little kids enjoy the show is exciting and funny," he says.

"I like the show because I watch all those cartoons, especially 'Goof Troop,'" says Robert. "I also think it's good because you can sing along if you want to."

> "I like the show because I watch all those cartoons."
>
> —Robert (age 8)

FANTASYLAND

Many of Walt Disney World's kiddie rides are in Fantasyland, but there are a few attractions that older kids and even grown-ups enjoy. We visited most of Fantasyland's rides during the 3 P.M. Main Street parade—and we suggest you do the same. These attractions are very popular, but the lines are much shorter while most people are at the parade. So it's a good idea to skip the parade one day to tour Fantasyland, and use the time to go on the rides. Catch the parade on another day.

Cinderella's Golden Carrousel

Just about all of the attractions at Walt Disney World were designed and built by Imagineers. The carousel is one exception. It was built around 1917. Imagineers discovered it in New Jersey,

Don't Forget

If the line is long, save the carousel for another time.

" You can never grow too old for a carousel. "

—Lissy (age 11)

scenes from *Cinderella*. While you ride, enjoy famous Disney tunes including "Zip-A-Dee-Doo-Dah," "When You Wish Upon A Star," and "Chim-Chim-Cheree."

"I think you can never grow too old for a carousel," says Lissy. "The horses are beautiful and the music makes it great."

Robert agrees. "I love the carousel and I love the music. I think people of any age would like it."

Some of the other kids feel differently. "It's very boring and babyish," says Ashley. David agrees. "I think it goes on forever and it's boring," he says.

Nita found a way to make the ride more fun for everyone by clapping in time with the music. "It's boring, so that's why I started clapping," she says. Brian thinks that helps a lot. "I didn't like it until we all started clapping," he says. "Then it was kind of fun."

Karyn thinks the carousel is a nice, relaxing ride. "It's fun when we all were clapping, and it's nice to just rest for a little while."

All the kids agree that they wouldn't wait in a long line to ride.

where it was once part of an amusement park.

When you climb on a horse for your ride on the carousel, be sure to notice that each one is different. And remember to look up at the ceiling and its hand-painted

Mad Tea Party

The idea for the oversize teacups that spin wildly through this ride was taken from a scene from *Alice In Wonderland*. In it, the Mad Hatter throws himself a tea party to celebrate his un-birthday. On the Mad Tea Party ride, you control how fast the cups spin by turning the big wheel in the center. The more you turn, the more you spin. Or you can just sit back and spin slowly with the movement of the ride. It may be difficult while you're spinning, but try to take a peek at the little mouse who keeps popping out of the big teapot in the center.

"**You can go as fast or as slow as you want.**"

—Brian (age 12)

"It's a very good ride and it really makes you dizzy," says Nita. Brian agrees. "I wish it would go even faster, but it's good that you can go as fast or as slow as you want," he says.

Robert says, "The ride is really cool. I think it should have power steering, though."

For the best ride, David suggests that everyone in the cup try to work together. "You have to coordinate," he says. "Sometimes you can go faster if fewer people work at spinning the wheel."

All the kids agree about two things: The ride is too short (it lasts about two minutes), and it would be better if there were a button to push instead of the wheel to spin. "Your arms get tired after a while," says Lissy, "but the teacups are always fun."

Dumbo, the Flying Elephant

Just like the star of the movie *Dumbo*, the elephants at this attraction fly. You can climb aboard and take a short ride (about two minutes) up and over Fantasyland. A button lets you control the up and down movement of the elephant. Timothy Mouse, who becomes Dumbo's manager in the movie, sits on top of a mirrored ball in the middle of the flying elephants. The ride received a fresh coat of colorful paint not too long ago, and more Dumbos were added so that more people can ride at once.

Many of the kids agree that this ride is more fun for younger kids from ages 3 to 8. But they all find something to like, and think it would be fun to go on with a younger brother or sister.

"I think it's great for younger kids," says Karyn. "It's pretty boring for kids my age, though." Brian also recommends it for younger kids. "It's not a bad ride and I think little kids would love it," he says. Anna thinks "it's way too short. But if you don't wait in line too long, it's fun to go on."

Lindsay says, "It needs to be new and improved again. But it's fun to control how high you go." Robert likes "to go up really high. I think some little kids might be scared of the height, though."

Danielle loves it. "It has the appearance of a child's ride, but it's fun for everyone," she says. Tate agrees. "Most people think it's just for little kids, but it's fun."

> "It's fun for everyone."
>
> —Danielle (age 11)

Peter Pan's Flight

Swoop and soar through scenes that tell the story of how Wendy, Michael, and John get sprinkled with pixie dust, head for "the second star to the right and straight on till morning," and fly off to Never Land with Tinkerbell. Along the way they meet up with Princess Tiger Lilly, the evil Captain Hook, and his sidekick Mr. Smee. Near the end of the trip, there's a beautiful scene of London at night. Notice that the cars on the streets really move. Also, watch out for the crocodile who's about to eat Captain Hook.

When you first board your pirate ship, it seems like you're riding on a track on the ground. Once you get going the track is actually above you, so you feel like you're really flying.

"I love this ride and how it makes you feel like you can fly," says Robert. "I especially like the part at the end with the crocodile."

Ashley thinks "the city scene is neat with all the cars going up and down. I also like how it's so dark."

Lissy enjoys "how you fly over all the scenes from the story. I really like the music, too." Nita says, "I think it really brings out the kid in you."

David points out that Peter Pan's Flight is different from all the other rides because "you're hooked from the top instead of being on a track below you." He adds, "I never get tired of this ride."

Brian likes all the details, like the costumes and colors of the characters. "I like how it shows parts from the movie *Peter Pan*," he says, "and I like it that you're flying instead of riding on the ground."

> " It really brings out the kid in you. "
>
> —Nita (age 14)

It's A Small World

This is a boat ride through a mini wonderland. Boats take you slowly through several large rooms where beautiful, Audio-Animatronics dolls represent different parts of the world. There are wooden soldiers, cancan dancers, Dutch children, Greek dancers, snake charmers, hot-air balloon fliers, leprechauns, bagpipers, and many more. There's even a jungle scene with hippos, giraffes, and monkeys.

All this colorful scenery is set to the song "It's A Small World," which plays over and over again. Pay attention to the detailed costumes on the dolls, and try to guess which country they're from. There are usually two lines at this attraction, and the one on the left is almost always shorter.

Pick the line on the left—it's almost always shorter.

"I love all the costumes, the different dolls, and the customs," says Karyn. "Every time you go, you see something new." Nita says, "The costumes are adorable, and I like the expressions on the dolls. But the ride is too slow. If it had a few dips it would be better."

Lissy agrees that the ride is a little slow, but "it's really pretty and there are so many neat things to look at that it doesn't matter."

Ashley thinks the song gets a little tiring. "I really like the costumes and cultures, but the song just keeps going over and over."

Brian says, "The figures are neat, and I love all the colors and costumes. The ride should be shorter, though."

As for David, "I don't hate it, but I think it's better for younger kids," he says.

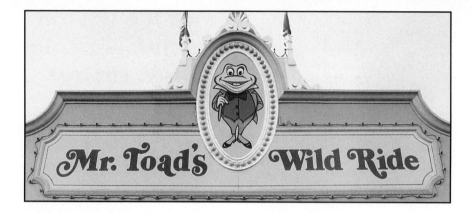

Mr. Toad's Wild Ride

Mr. Toad is not a very good driver. So when you hop into one of his cars heading to "Nowhere in Particular," you're in for a wild trip. The cars go zigging and zagging around sharp turns. You crash through a fireplace, just miss being hit by a falling suit of armor, go through haystacks and barn doors into a chicken coop, and then ride down a railroad track on a collision course with a speeding train.

Most of the kids agree that Mr. Toad's Wild Ride is for younger kids, although there are a few scary moments that might frighten them.

"It's good for younger kids," says Karyn. "It's pretty boring for someone my age."

David agrees that it's a kiddie ride. "Some of the characters are funny, but it's really just for younger kids," he says. "I don't like that the characters are all made out of cardboard."

But Lissy thinks the scenery is "neat and I like how they have everything moving. When I saw the train coming, it was a little scary," she says. Robert agrees, "It sort of scared me a little bit."

Brian thinks the soundtrack is too loud. "The ride is good for younger kids, but the noise might scare them."

> "Some of the characters are funny, but it's really just for younger kids."
>
> —David (age 13)

Snow White's Adventures

As you travel through this attraction, you see some of the scariest parts from the story of *Snow White and the Seven Dwarfs*. The ride has been updated to add Snow White to most of the scenes. There also are Audio-Animatronics dwarfs. At the end of the ride, they wave to Snow White and her prince.

There are lots of turns, and that witch seems to be around each one of them. During most of the ride it's very dark, so it can get pretty scary—especially for younger children.

The kids agree that this attraction doesn't fit well into any age category. It's very scary for young children and a little boring for older kids.

"At least Snow White is in more of it now, but I still think it's too scary for little kids," says Karyn. "If it's going to be a kiddie ride, there should be more happy parts in it." Tate says, "I expected something more."

Ashley likes the ride but thinks "it would be too scary for young kids because the witch hops out so close to you."

Brian likes that some scenes are like the movie, but he agrees, "Little kids would be terrified seeing the wicked witch."

Dawna says, "I like how we moved from scene to scene in our car. Still, I wouldn't wait in a long line for this ride."

"The witch hops out so close to you."
—Ashley (age 11)

Legend of The Lion King

Walt Disney's smash hit comes to life in Legend of The Lion King. This show uses animation, life-size puppets, special effects, and music to make you part of the world of Simba.

You start in the pre-show area, where you meet Rafiki, the wise baboon who narrates the story. Soon the doors to the theater open, and you step into the scene of the Circle of Life. The sun rises over Pride Rock as Mufasa tells his son, Simba, that he will always have his father with him. The characters are fully automated puppets, whose heads, ears, and feet move, and whose mouths open and shut when they speak.

As the story continues, you meet other characters from the movie and experience some of its most dramatic scenes. You're there when Mufasa is trampled and when Simba discovers that his father is dead. You see the evil Scar make Simba believe it's his

"I was mesmerized the whole time."

—Dawna (age 11)

fault his father has died. You go with Simba when he leaves the kingdom and finds freedom with Timon and Pumbaa. Later, you watch as he falls in love with Nala. When Rafiki convinces Simba it's time to go back to the kingdom, you return with him as he takes his place as The Lion King.

The special effects, like mists and winds, make it seem as if you're really in the jungle. During the stampede scene, feel the theater rumble as Mufasa is trampled by the wildebeests.

All the kids think this is a great show. "This has to be the best show anywhere," Dawna says. "I was mesmerized the whole time." Lindsay calls it "a good performance, with all of your favorite songs and characters from the movie." Karyn says it's a "must see." Even Tate, who's never

seen *The Lion King* "thoroughly enjoyed it."

If you're a Lion King fan, don't miss the Fantasy Faire gift shop outside the show. Everything is based on the hit movie, so you're sure to find something you like.

Skyway to Tomorrowland

Get a bird's-eye view of the Magic Kingdom on the cable cars that run overhead between Fantasyland and Tomorrowland.

"This is fun," says Lindsay. "You get a really good view of the park and you can take pictures." Brad agrees. "It's cool going up in the air. You get to see everything."

Anna suggests that you "walk if the line is longer than ten minutes. It's silly to wait if you can get where you're going faster." But Adam says, "It's nice to ride and rest your feet."

Board at Tomorrowland, where the lines are usually shorter.

Dawna and Danielle both think the ride feels a little like a ski lift. Dawna points out that "obviously, it's not a good ride if you're afraid of heights."

Kids who remember **20,000 Leagues Under the Sea** should know that it's closed until further notice.

notes

TOMORROWLAND

Tomorrowland was designed as Walt Disney World's version of the future. But the present keeps catching up, so most of the land has been updated to include some brand-new attractions. One thing is still the same—Space Mountain, which is among the Magic Kingdom's most popular rides. Some of the newest attractions are Alien Encounter, Astro Orbiter, and The Timekeeper.

Space Mountain

Roller coaster fans will want to head straight for Space Mountain and its fast, winding trip through the galaxy. You must be at least 44 inches tall to ride. You travel in a rocket, in the dark (but not pitch black), with stars and meteors all around.

The kids agree that the turns and pretty steep dips of Space Mountain make for a great ride.

Justin thinks "it's fun because you never know what's going to happen next." All the special effects make the ride even better for Brad. "The speeding lights look really neat," he says.

Once you get inside the mountain, you choose between two lines. Karyn thinks "sitting on the left is better because there are more dips and turns."

Nita has a warning for kids who aren't sure if they want to go on: "It goes too fast for somebody like me. I'm not a roller coaster person, and I felt like I was about to fall out when it went sideways." Another bit of good advice from Lindsay: "Make sure you don't go on this ride before or after you eat."

The ride lasts just over 2½ minutes. "Waiting in line you think 'The ride is only two minutes long! That's not long enough,'" says Lissy. "Then you get on and two minutes seems too long," she says.

All the kids agree that the ride is

Don't Forget

Never eat right before going on Space Mountain.

"good scary." Anything "bad scary" happened only in their imaginations.

Anna says, "The ride rattles a lot. I wish that there were sides to the cars." But don't worry: The roller coaster is perfectly safe to go on as many times as you want. As Tate says, "Just one word—again!"

The **Tomorrowland Power & Light Co**. is a video arcade located at the exit of Space Mountain. It's a great place to wait if you don't ride. One of the most popular games is the Sega Virtua Formula race car. "You get to sit in a simulated car," says Dawna. "It's almost like really driving in a race against everyone around you." As at most other arcades, you'll have to pay to play. The race car game costs $1.50 a turn.

Alien Encounter

Visitors from another planet invite you to watch them demonstrate their company's new teleporter. This is a high-tech device that can beam people through space. To show you exactly how it works, the visitors say they'll beam their company president from their planet right into this theater in the Magic Kingdom. But something goes wrong: An ugly alien arrives instead and escapes into the audience.

That's the story behind Alien Encounter, the Magic Kingdom's scariest attraction. Special effects play a big part in this new show. There's smoke, sparks, and lots of sounds designed to make things even more frightening.

" The scariest show I've ever seen. "

—Dawna (age 11)

On our visit, we saw a preview of Alien Encounter. Since then, Disney's Imagineers have added a lot of special effects to make the show even more realistic and even scarier.

The kids like this show, but stress that it's not for everyone— especially younger kids. "It doesn't seem like a Disney show. If you like those scary things, it's fine," says Karyn. "But if you're like me, you definitely don't want to try it."

Lindsay is just the opposite. She likes horror movies and other scary things. "I love this show," she says. "The special effects are really cool. It's neat how they make the creature disappear and then reappear somewhere else."

Dawna calls this "the scariest show I've ever seen. I probably was screaming three-fourths of the time. It feels like the Alien is right behind you." She also doesn't recommend the show for younger kids. "I think kids under 8 would get nightmares or start crying in the middle of it. It's very dark in there," she says.

The Timekeeper

Travel through time with Timekeeper, an Audio-Animatronics robot who's your host for this attraction. With his assistant, 9-Eye, Timekeeper takes you on a tour of the past and the future. You experience the ice age and see the creation of the Eiffel Tower. You meet a talented, young musician named Mozart. You even get to spend time with Jules Verne and H.G. Wells, two of the originators of science fiction.

9-Eye is a female droid whose oversize head is filled with nine cameras. She travels from century to century, sending back pictures that fill the nine screens of the Circle-Vision 360 theater. The movie makes it seem as if you're moving through time with her.

"This made me dizzy but still is sort of neat," says Lindsay. "I felt like it was more than just a movie." Dawna agrees. "I felt as if I was actually moving," she says. "This is a very funny show. If there's a long line, it would definitely be worth the wait."

Tate also really enjoys this. He likes that Timekeeper is played by the very funny actor Robin Williams. (The other stars in the show are Rhea Perlman, Jeremy Irons, and Michel Piccoli). Tate says, "The antics of Robin Williams make this attraction what it is." Karyn also likes Robin Williams. "But I don't think I would wait in a long line for it. If I had time and there wasn't a crowd, I'd go on it," she says.

" I felt like it was more than just a movie. "

—Lindsay (age 9)

Walt Disney's Carousel of Progress

"It's a down-to-earth look at how the American family has progressed over the years."

—Tate (age 13)

An Audio-Animatronics family stars in scenes that show how electricity has improved American life. This exhibit made its debut at the New York World's Fair in 1964. There's a new scene at the end predicting how the family might live in the year 2000.

The show is called Carousel of Progress because you travel around the scenes in a circle, just like a carousel. Sometimes it's hard to tell if it's the stage or the audience that's moving.

Most of the kids enjoy this show. "I really appreciate the story," says Tate. "It's a down-to-earth look at how the American family has progressed over the years."

Anna finds it "a good way to learn. I think it's cool when they

say, in the early scenes, how 'that will never happen,' and we know that it already has."

Adam likes "how we learn about all the inventions that were created in the years past."

Danielle notices that "the sets look very realistic. It's interesting going through history that way." Brad's favorite is "the part at the end when the Granny is playing the virtual reality game. It's neat how they go from year to year, but the last scene is the best."

Delta Dreamflight

Trace the history of aviation on a journey that takes you from man's first attempts at flight through the many advances in technology. The start of the trip features a giant pop-up book to show you that the story of flight is about to unfold. As you ride along, you see two movie sequences that make you feel like you're part of the action.

You also see a full-size section of the first type of airplane to cross the Atlantic Ocean. Notice how luxurious travel was in those days. Look at the scenes of foreign places that air travel makes it possible to visit.

Near the end of the ride, you pass through a jet engine. Special effects re-create the engine's rotation and make you feel like you're spinning. The last scene is another pop-up book showing London and New York.

The kids enjoy parts of this ride, but think it needs a narrator. "An announcer to explain all the things you're seeing would be good," says Taran. "This is a learning ride, so they should teach more."

The kids give high marks to the movie sequence that makes you feel like you're flying and to the spinning engine. Brad says, "When you're supposed to be in the airplane, it really feels like you're flying." Robert agrees. "When you're watching the movie, it's like you're actually there," he says. "I like the big pop-up books, too."

Lindsay says, "I thought we would take off and go fast. But

> ## "It really feels like you're flying."
> ### —Brad (age 10)

it's really slow." Danielle thinks that's the way it should be. "Then you can watch all the scenery," she says.

For Brian, the ride gets better as it goes along. "When it first starts, it goes so slowly. But then it feels like you're flying and going much faster than you really are. That's pretty neat," he says.

All the kids agree with Anna: "If there is a line, don't wait. But if you have the time, it's okay."

Grand Prix Raceway

You can drive your own car (as long as you're 52 inches tall) on a lap around the racetrack at the Grand Prix. The cars travel along a track, but it's not as easy as it looks. Even expert drivers have some trouble. The cars are real and are powered by gasoline. They have rack-and-pinion steering and disc brakes, and travel at about seven miles per hour.

"No matter how perfectly you drive, it always goes off the track," says Nita.

Brian agrees. "It feels like you don't have very good control of the car and you don't go very fast," he says.

Some of the kids really enjoy driving their own cars. "I love it. I thought it went pretty fast and I like having my own car," says Robert. Ashley agrees. "It's fun driving my own car. I think they should have it without the track."

David and Karyn think the ride gets boring once you've done it a few times. "I like the ride, but I wish they didn't have the track in the middle. It gets a little boring after a while," says David.

Karyn agrees. "It used to be one of my favorites, but it's a little boring now," she says. "I don't think very young kids would like it because they can't drive, and that's the whole fun of it."

> " It's fun driving my own car. "
>
> —Ashley (age 11)

Astro Orbiter

At the center of Tomorrowland is Rockettower Plaza—a tower that glows with colorful flashing lights. At the top is Astro Orbiter, a ride with giant, spinning rockets. They take you past whirling planets and give you a great view of Tomorrowland.

"This is one of the few rides that everyone will really enjoy," says Tate. "It's fast, but not to the point that it's too scary." Dawna agrees. "It's a good ride for little kids because you can control whether your ship goes up or down," she says. "People who don't have the stomach for Space Mountain can go here because it still has the

space theme." Lindsay likes "that you get to go up in an elevator to take the ride. When you go up high in your rocket, you get a pretty good view."

But to Karyn, "It's just like rides at the fair or at any other theme park. I think this would be more for younger kids."

The **Tomorrowland Transit Authority** travels alongside or through most of the land's attractions. If you're not sure about going on Space Mountain, the view from here can help you decide. It's also interesting to note that the ride runs on a motor with no moving parts. That means it doesn't give off any pollution.

"If people want to get off their feet, this is the place to be," says Dawna. "It's somewhat entertaining and relaxing. And you can see a lot of Tomorrowland in a very short time."

If you're dying to ride the **Skyway** cable cars that travel from Tomorrowland to Fantasyland and back, this is your best chance. The lines at the Tomorrowland station are much shorter, so board here.

AWESOME
(See at Least Twice)

Space Mountain

Splash Mountain

Big Thunder
Mountain Railroad

Haunted Mansion

Legend of The Lion King

REALLY COOL
(Don't Miss)

Grand Prix Raceway

Peter Pan's Flight

Mickey's Starland

Pirates of the
Caribbean

Carousel of Progress

Alien Encounter

*My visit to the Magic
Kingdom will include . . .*

COOL
(Check it Out)

It's A Small World

Jungle Cruise

Swiss Family Treehouse

Mad Tea Party

Mr. Toad's Wild Ride

Cinderella's Golden Carrousel

The Hall of Presidents

Dumbo, The Flying Elephant

Skyway

The Timekeeper

Tomorrowland Transit Authority

Astro Orbiter

YAWN
(Save For Last)

Walt Disney World Railroad

Country Bear Jamboree

Snow White's Adventures

Delta Dreamflight

Main Street Cinema

Tropical Serenade

Tom Sawyer Island

Epcot

Epcot, which stands for "Experimental Prototype Community of Tomorrow," is divided into two sections: Future World and World Showcase. On one side of the park, there is a very large lake known as World Showcase Lagoon.

When you first enter Epcot, you are in Future World. The pavilions here have exhibits and rides that explore communication, energy, imagination, the ocean, agriculture, and health. These topics may sound a little dull, but with just a few exceptions, the kids really enjoy them.

World Showcase is a group of countries—Canada, the United Kingdom, France, Morocco, Japan, the United States, Italy, Germany, China, Norway, and Mexico—all arranged around the lagoon. Each Epcot country includes copies of famous landmarks to make you feel as if you're visiting the real thing.

There are a few movies to see, plus a ride through Norway and Mexico. But mostly, World Showcase is designed to give you the flavor of the different cultures. The people who work at the pavilions and in the restaurants and shops are actually from the represented countries.

FUTURE WORLD

Although Future World seems like it's just educational, there are lots of things for kids to explore. Start out at Wonders of Life, the kids' favorite pavilion. Be sure to check out all of the hands-on activities there and at Innoventions, Sea Base Alpha in The Living Seas pavilion, and Image Works at the Journey Into Imagination pavilion. Save the rest of Future World for the afternoon, when it's less crowded.

INNOVENTIONS

Here's your chance to try games, computers, and other inventions, most of them so new they're not for sale in any store. You see the latest appliances and electronics from some of the world's best known companies.

Sega, LEGO, IBM, AT&T, General Electric, Apple, and General Motors all have things to share and show at Innoventions. Best of all, these aren't just ideas or things that might happen. Some of the products are available right now, while others will be on the market during the next couple of years.

"This is one of the coolest places for kids," says Tate. "You should schedule at least a couple of hours to get the full effect."

Interesting inventions are brought in every three months to keep up with the newest ideas. That means the exhibits may be different during your visit. But no matter when you come, you'll get a taste of the future.

Karyn's favorite exhibit is the virtual reality in the Eclectronics area. When we visited, she got to try a virtual guitar that makes anyone sound like a musician. The new virtual museum exhibit lets you see a famous chuch in Italy without actually going there.

Dawna is amazed by the video games. "There are more here than I've ever seen," she says, "and they're all free." She also likes the house of the future, with its appliances to make home life easier. "The inventors have figured out how we can use a remote to open windows and even prepare breakfast," she says. "You could be miles away from your house and turn on your oven."

All the kids like the Walt Disney Imagineering Laboratory, which shows you something guests have never seen before—Imagineers at work on future attractions. "This is one cool idea," says Lindsay. "There's nothing else like it."

During our visit, Imagineers were working on a flying carpet ride that uses virtual reality, animation, and computer graphics to create a flying experience like Aladdin's.

Four guest pilots get to test the ride and the virtual reality helmet. Those who aren't chosen to ride can watch the pilots in action. Dawna was a test pilot. "It's a lot of fun," she says. "I had to wear a funny hat and sit on a bicycle-like thing." Tate thinks "it's very cool to see the visual effects, even if you don't get to be a pilot."

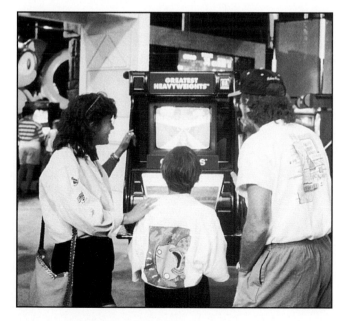

There's lots more to do and see at Innoventions. If you're not sure where to start, try the multimedia show starring Bill Nye, the Science Guy. He tells you what to expect and explains the scientific principles behind many of the inventions. Most of the kids find the movie a little boring, but admit it's a good way to learn what Innoventions has to offer.

SPACESHIP EARTH

The symbol of Epcot is the giant silver ball that you can see from almost anywhere in the park. Inside the ball is the Spaceship Earth Show, a ride through the history of communications. You travel in a "time machine" from the days of Cro-Magnon man (30,000 to 40,000 years ago) to the future. The highlight comes when your time machine reaches the top of the dome and you're in the middle of the communications revolution. There are some great special effects, including colorful laser beams.

The older kids like this attraction more than the younger ones. Ashley remembers that she didn't like the ride when she was younger, but "now it's much more interesting."

"Being inside the ball is cool," says Karyn. "Knowing that during the whole ride you're actually inside the huge thing you see outside is amazing."

Nita says, "The details are great, like the monk who is snoring. I especially love the Greek scene."

The details make the ride a lot more interesting. Look at the real hieroglyphics in the Egyptian scene. Notice, in the scene with the printing press, that the keys really work. Also, watch Michelangelo's arm as he paints the ceiling of the Sistine Chapel.

If you've been on this ride before, you may be in for a surprise. It's been updated, and the new scenes are a big hit with the kids. "They show how one day we'll be able to use virtual reality for a field trip instead of actually going to a certain place," Dawna says. Karyn also likes taking a look at the future. "My favorite part is the video phones," she says. "I really like all the changes. They make the ride a little more exciting."

After the ride, check out the new

AT&T Global Neighborhood exhibit. It offers lots of fun, hands-on ways to learn more about communications networks.

59

Don't go to Spaceship Earth first thing in the morning because that's when it's most crowded.

THE LIVING SEAS

Explore the deep waters of the Caribbean Sea in the world's largest aquarium. There are more than 5,000 sea creatures, including sharks, dolphins, barracuda, angelfish, sea lions, and many more. Your sea exploration begins in the waiting area, where there are samples of old wet suits worn by the first divers. Then you see a video presentation and a movie. Next, you get on board a "hydrolator" to go down to explore the coral reef. Ask your parents if the hydrolator takes them deep underground. Then tell them they've actually traveled less than an inch.

After a ride through the aquarium, you are left off at Sea Base Alpha. This is your chance to take a closer look at the creatures of the sea and to try out the many hands-on exhibits.

"Living Seas is really cool," says Robert. "I thought my ears popped in the hydrolator. It feels like you're going way down to the bottom of

"It feels like you're going way down to the bottom of the sea."

—Robert (age 8)

she says, "but I prefer to see the real animals."

Taran and Robert agree. "The manatees are really cool," Taran says. And Robert adds, "I saw a spotted eagle ray, which is like a stingray. That was cool, too."

the sea, even though you're only going down three-quarters of an inch."

David says, "It's fun learning about the different kinds of fish in the ocean."

Brian likes the hands-on exhibits. "You can put your arms in a diving suit and try to move like you're in the ocean," he says.

Nita and Taran tried the diving suit test together. "We didn't pass," Nita says. "It's really difficult to do things in a suit like that. It shows how hard it is for real divers." Taran explains, "I reached out and pulled the lever, but nothing happened. It's really hard."

Karyn "just loves the manatees. The rest of the exhibits are okay,"

THE LAND

This pavilion focuses on one of everybody's favorite subjects—food. There's a boat ride through a greenhouse, a funny show about food, special guided tours, plus a movie about the environment featuring Simba, Timon, and Pumbaa from *The Lion King*.

Living with the Land

Set out on a journey that takes you through a simulated rain forest, a desert, and a prairie. See experimental technology that's used to grow plants in different environments. There's a desert farm with a drip irrigation system and an area where they're experimenting to see if fish can be grown like farm products.

The boat ride scores high marks with some of the kids. "It teaches about all of the different land regions," says Dawna. Brian likes that "it shows how plants can grow in soils like desert sand."

Adam says, "It's a long ride, but very worthwhile. It's neat how you get to see growing plants in the greenhouses." Danielle agrees. "I don't eat meat, so I like seeing how the food I eat is grown."

Lindsay loves this ride. "The greenhouses are amazing," she says. Justin learned a lot on this boat trip. "Before, I just knew that you put a seed into the ground and it grows. On the ride I learned more detail than that." Anna did not like this as much, but says, "It does show us new ways to make the best of our earth."

> "The greenhouses are amazing."
> —Lindsay (age 9)

Food Rocks

Here's a rock concert with a message about good nutrition. Popular musicians, who have been turned into foods, perform favorite songs with new lyrics. Füd Wrapper, modeled after rap singer Tone Loc, is the host of this funny show. The introduction is a "heavy metal" song performed by four-foot-tall kitchen utensils.

Other performers include Chubby Cheddar, Neil Moussaka, Pita Gabriel, and The Refrigerator Police, led by a milk carton wearing sunglasses.

In the pre-show area, there are murals with facts about food. Giant "smell boxes" can be found around the room. Open one and get a strong whiff of garlic, chocolate, coffee, bacon, orange, or seafood. Dawna points out the carpeting, with its pattern of forks, knives, and spoons.

The kids like the show, but think it's best for a younger audience. "This is a clever idea and a good way to teach kids about nutrition and the right foods to eat," says Lindsay. Tate calls Food Rocks "a cute show for little kids." Dawna likes "the Füd Wrapper and all of the other singers. I wouldn't go to this right before or after eating because it makes you feel guilty for eating food that's not good for you," she says.

Most of the kids like the names of the performers and the songs they sing. But sometimes it's hard to make out the lyrics. "I can't understand the words of the songs," Lindsay says. "I do think their names are clever, though."

Circle of Life

Simba, Timon, and Pumbaa are together again in this movie on protecting the environment, shown in the Harvest Theater. In the opening scene, Simba, king of the Pridelands, is next to a watering hole. All of a sudden he hears "Timber!" and is drenched by the splash of a fallen tree. Simba soon discovers why the tree was cut down. Timon and Pumbaa are clearing the savanna to build the Hakuna Matata Lakeside Village.

Simba remembers what his father taught him about caring for the land, and shares it with his friends. He tells them a story about a creature who sometimes forgets that everything is connected in the great Circle of Life. "That creature," Simba says, "is man."

The movie wasn't open in time for our visit, but with Timon and Pumbaa, it's a good bet that you'll

Kids (and parents) who are very interested in the environment can sign up for the **Greenhouse Tour**. This is an 45-minute guided tour of the growing areas at The Land pavilion. A new laboratory shows some exciting technology, including how scientists can transfer genes from one plant to another. There's an extra charge of $5 for adults and $3 for kids ages 3 to 9. You'll need reservations. Make them as early as possible at the tour podium near the Green Thumb Emporium shop.

like this attraction. It mixes animation and live footage to show some of the environmental problems we face—and how we can fix them.

JOURNEY INTO IMAGINATION

Your host for this pavilion is Figment—a magical creature created from a lizard's body, a crocodile's nose, a steer's horns, two big yellow eyes, two small wings, and a pinch of childish delight. Figment is most often thought of as a baby dragon. He's so popular that he has become a mascot for Epcot.

Inside the pavilion is a ride through the wonders of the imagination, a hands-on activity center called Image Works, and a 3-D movie called *Honey, I Shrunk the Audience*. Outside the pavilion are the Leap Frog Fountains, whose streams of water leap from one garden to another in the most amazing way.

There are so many fun things to see and do in Image Works that the kids think you should plan on spending at least an hour at this pavilion.

Plan on spending at least an hour at this pavilion.

Journey Into Imagination Ride

Figment and his pal Dreamfinder lead you on a tour of the imagination. They show you how the five senses send messages to the brain to create dreams and ideas. This colorful ride is full of puffy clouds. It also has special effects like lasers and lightning.

About three-quarters of the way through the ride, you'll see a flash of light. Smile, because your picture is being taken. Look for it later, on a screen at the end of the ride.

"I like the little purple dragon," says Brad. "The ride is a little slow, but it's still cool."

Lindsay thinks the scenery is "very creative. You keep seeing the dragon and what he's imagining." Dawna agrees, saying, "The scenery is fantastic."

Anna's favorite part is that "they show you all the cool things you can do with art, like the sparkles, holograms, paints, and lights."

But Adam thinks the ride is too long. "I like the characters, but it's a little boring," he says. Tate agrees. "I think younger kids would like it best, though it does have a lot of neat stuff to look at."

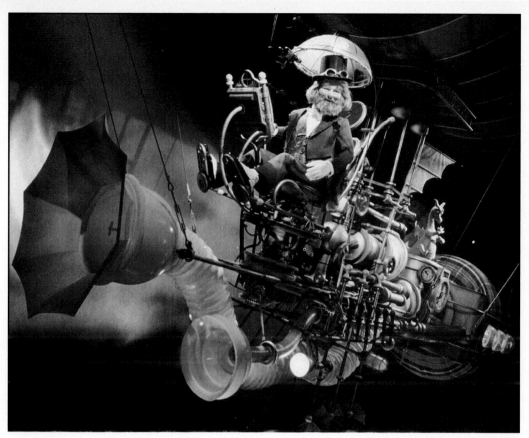

"You keep
seeing
the dragon
and what he's
imagining."
—Lindsay (age 9)

Image Works

Once you get inside Image Works, it may be hard to leave. This is heaven for kids, with lots of hands-on (and feet-on) activities. The Rainbow Corridor is a tunnel full of neon tubes in all the colors of the rainbow. Walk through it and you'll reach Stepping Tones, where you step on colored lights on the floor to trigger different sounds. It's especially fun when you're with lots of people and everyone joins in. Other activities include Lumia, a seven-foot plastic ball that shows swirling lights and colors when different voices are heard. The Magic Palette has a special stylus and a touch-sensitive screen that let you create all kinds of images using day-glo colors. At the Electronic Philharmonic you can conduct an orchestra by raising and lowering your hands.

"This place is totally awesome," says Lissy. "They have everything a kid could need to occupy herself."

Nita agrees. "There's so much to do. My favorite was directing the band." Ashley thinks "the lights and colors are really cool, and it's neat how many things there are to do."

David likes "having all the hands-on experiences. It's a very fun place," he says.

> "They have everything a kid could need to occupy herself."
>
> —Lissy (age 11)

Honey, I Shrunk the Audience

Inside the Imagination Theater is a movie based on *Honey, I Shrunk the Kids* and *Honey, I Blew Up the Kid*. This time, you're the one who gets shrunk, along with everyone else in the audience. You get attacked by 3-D mice, a 3-D lion, and a 3-D snake! The whole theater seems to shrink. Then Adam, the kid who was blown up in the movie, picks up the theater and carries it around. Somehow you're brought back to your actual size, but only after some unusual adventures.

"This is a very neat experience, and the special effects are really good," says Lindsay. "Some parts might be scary for little kids because the characters come out so far." Karyn thinks this movie is "too realistic. I was so scared when that snake came out!"

Tate says, "This attraction really gives you the feeling that you're shrinking. There's a neat twist at the end. The story is a little corny, though." Tate also offers this helpful hint: Keep the 3-D glasses on to get the most out of the movie. Dawna thinks "a lot of the 3-D looks like it's right in your face. I would recommend this if you liked the *Honey, I Shrunk the Kids* movie."

> " **This attraction really gives you the feeling that you're shrinking.**"
>
> —Tate (age 13)

Leap Frog Fountains

The arcing streams of water move from one garden plot to the next with no obvious pattern. That makes this area a highlight with kids of all ages.

"If you stand in the right place you can get totally wet," says Taran. "It's one of my favorite things." Robert agrees. "It's really cool and I like getting wet," he says.

Nita thinks it's neat "how the water jumps over your head." And Lissy likes the fountains because "they keep you on your toes. If you're hot, you can just stand there and get a refreshing break."

" **If you stand in the right place you can get totally wet.** "

—Taran (age 9)

Something New

If you've been to Future World before, you may remember the World of Motion. That ride will be closed during 1996 to make room for something even better. The new ride will take you on a thrilling trip through the motions of automobile testing. It will have cars that move quickly along a test track around curvy roads and up steep hills, and then slam on the brakes. Look for this new ride in mid-1997.

Sketch Pad

HORIZONS

Experience life in the future as you make your way through scenes showing a typical family in different environments. In the first scene, transportation and communication systems—such as holographic telephones and magnetic-levitation trains—help keep faraway family members close. The second scene shows robots harvesting fruits and vegetables that have been grown in a desert. The third scene takes place in a floating city, where schoolchildren take underwater field trips. The last setting is outer space, where family members stay in shape by playing games like zero-gravity basketball.

What happens at the end of the ride is up to you and the three other people in your car. Majority rules as you choose from land, sea, or space. Your car tilts back and vibrates, and special sound effects and close-up film sequences make you feel like you're moving very fast.

"I like the part where you choose where you want to go," says Nita.

"They show you how they think the future will be."
—Ashley (age 11)

You can choose your own ending, but majority rules in each car.

"It should be longer, though, because it's very interesting."

Ashley says, "In the underwater part, it's cool how everyone is eating. I like that they show you how they think the future will be."

Robert likes that the cars turn sideways "so you can really see everything."

David thinks there's a lot to see along the way. "There are many details, like the scuba class going by in the beginning, which you see again later on," he says. "I like learning about everyone's hopes for the future."

Note: Don't be surprised if this ride is closed during your visit. They'll be upgrading it on and off throughout the year. Look for a brand-new ride in the near future.

WONDERS OF LIFE

This pavilion has the kids' two favorite Epcot attractions— Body Wars, the rough ride through the human body, and Cranium Command, a great show about how the brain works. Also inside the building are many hands-on activities, *The Making of Me* (a movie about the birth of a baby), a cartoon show about health that stars Goofy, a stage show about anatomy, and much, much more. It's easy to spend a couple of hours here, so come early to beat the crowds.

Body Wars

Fasten your seatbelt for a very rough, bumpy ride through the human body. Before entering the vehicles, you are miniaturized for a special rescue mission to help a scientist who gets stuck while trying to remove a splinter. The ride takes place on a flight simulator, which is the same type of device used to train astronauts and pilots. Together, the simulator and the movie on the screen make you feel like you're really inside the body. The same technology is used at Star Tours at the Disney-MGM Studios, but Body Wars is a much rougher ride.

For Karyn, "It's a little too bumpy. I do like all the special effects, but it's too jerky," she says. Brian feels the same way. "You really get jerked around too much, and I don't like that kind

> ## "For the roughest ride, try to sit in the back."
> —Nita (age 14)

Cranium Command

Imagine that you're a pilot. But instead of flying an airplane, you pilot the brain of a 12-year-old boy. That's what happens to Buzzy in this attraction. The first part of the show takes place outside the theater, in a preview area. There you see a funny movie that explains how Buzzy gets his job. Then you go into the theater—and inside the brain with Buzzy. You watch as he tries to get all the parts of the brain to work together.

"You think it will be a little story about the brain or something," says Taran. "Instead it turns out to be a really cool thing."

Lissy agrees. "I like it a lot because you learn different things about the brain and how it works with the rest of your body—and you have a lot of fun at the same time." And Karyn thinks that "it's very educational as well as cute and funny."

Be sure to pay attention to that first movie. Dawna says, "I like the funny animation at the beginning. It explains what will happen in the theater." Robert points out, "If you didn't see the pre-show, you'd go crazy trying to figure out what was going on."

of ride," he says.

The ride is still a favorite for most of the kids. "I love it," says Robert. "It's not scary at all, and it's cool and fun the way you go through the body." Ashley agrees. "I really like bumpy rides, so I like this one a lot."

Nita has been on it a few times "and I still like it. For the roughest ride, try to sit in the back," she advises.

"You really have to hold on to the arms of the seats or you get thrashed around," warns Taran. "I think it should take longer to get from the heart to the brain, or that you should go all the way down to the feet and then bounce up to the brain," he adds.

Don't worry if some people in your group don't want to go on Body Wars. There are plenty of things for them to do at Wonders of Life. And you can meet them when you get off the ride.

The brain in Cranium Command belongs to a boy named Bobby. Once inside the brain, you see Buzzy trying to pilot Bobby through a day at school. "It's very comical," Tate says. "I really can relate to some of the things that happen to the boy in the story because he's about my age."

HOT TIP:

Be sure to pay attention to the pre-show.

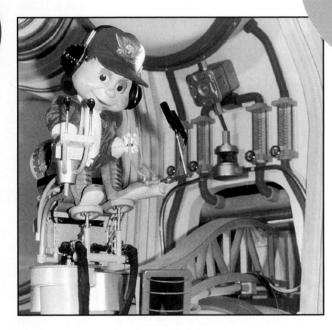

Anna says, "I recommend this to all ages, especially teenagers."

Brad likes how the parts of the brain are each played by a different character. "I like all the stars, like the guy in the stomach from 'Cheers,' and Hans and Franz pumping the heart." He notices that "the left brain would always make things realistic." Robert adds that "the left brain is totally logical and the right brain is crazy."

Lindsay advises that you pay attention. "I didn't know what to look at first. There's so much going on." All the details make this a show you can enjoy more than once.

The show helped all the kids understand how the brain works. Lindsay says, "This is funny and a perfect way to learn about your body." Besides, as Brian points out, "It's a lot of fun to see all the different things that go on in our brain each day."

The kids agree that Cranium Command is one attraction that's kind of hidden in the Wonders of Life pavilion. None of them had ever seen it—even though some had been to the World before. So don't miss it!

Fitness Fairgrounds

The lobby of the Wonders of Life pavilion has so many hands-on activities, the kids think you can spend at least an hour here. There are Wonder Cycles, which are computerized bicycles that allow you to watch film footage while riding. In the Coach's Corner, tennis, baseball, and golf swings are analyzed, and you get tips for a better game. The Sensory Fun House has many different hands-on choices. The kids enjoy trying to guess what certain objects are without being able to see them.

"There's tons of stuff to do,"

There are many other activities at the Wonders of Life pavilion. **Goofy About Health** is a cartoon show about how Goofy goes from being a sloppy-living guy to a health-conscious fellow. At the **Anacomical Players Theater**, you see a corny but informative show about good health. **The Making of Me** is a movie about the birth of a baby with real scenes in a hospital. A must.

says Dawna. "I like the bicycles. At the end it tells you how many miles you've gone."

Adam made a good showing at the Coach's Corner. "I really like the baseball critique. It's neat how they can tell you what you're doing wrong," he says.

Justin likes that "you can touch everything. It's so much fun." Lindsay agrees. "It's really fun and different from other places."

Anna likes "how you can experiment hands-on, and you can figure things out for yourself. With the bright colors and decorations, this is the perfect Walt Disney World attraction."

UNIVERSE OF ENERGY

This pavilion takes a look at the many ways in which energy was originally created—and how it's created today. It includes two films, an animated movie, and a ride through prehistoric times complete with huge dinosaurs. When you first enter the pavilion, you see a film about the types of energy in use today. Then an animated movie shows you what prehistoric Earth looked like and how fossil fuels were created.

The theater seats break up into several sections and take you into the prehistoric world of the animated movie. You travel through lots of fog, past huge trees, real-looking lava, and

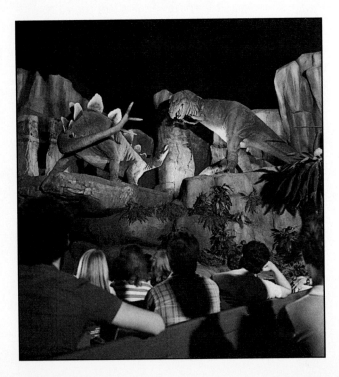

"**The best part of the ride is when it's over.**"

—Robert (age 8)

several types of dinosaurs, including a brontosaurus, an allosaurus, an elasmosaurus, and pteranodons. These are some of the largest animals of their type ever to be made.

The vehicles then move into another theater, where you see a movie about the future of energy exploration. This movie lasts 12½ minutes—and seems even longer. That's one reason this attraction is not a favorite with the kids. "The dinosaurs are okay, but the last movie is way too long," Nita says. Ashley agrees. "I think the whole thing is very boring," she says.

"I like the dinosaurs," says David. "But the movies are so boring that I grew restless." And Robert thinks "the best part of the ride is when it's over."

Note: Changes will be made to this ride in 1996, so it may be closed during your visit. Right now, the kids rate it a "yawn." That could change after the improvements are made.

n o t e s

WORLD SHOWCASE

Touring the shops and attractions in the different World Showcase pavilions is interesting for kids. But most agree that they would like more things geared for them. Dawna points out that "the pavilions with a ride or movie are more fun. I'd also like to stop and talk to the people who work there about their countries." Lindsay wanted to take a guided tour. "A tour guide could tell you all about the countries. Each one has lots of details, and some of them make you feel like you're really there," she says.

CANADA

The beauty of America's northern neighbor is on display at this pavilion. There's a rocky mountain, a rushing stream, beautiful gardens, and a totem pole. The highlight at the Canada pavilion is a movie, *O Canada!* It was filmed using a technology called Circle-Vision 360, so the Canadian scenery surrounds you completely. The theater has no seats. You stand, so it's easy to turn around and see the whole picture.

The movie takes a coast-to-coast look at Canada, including scenes of skiers, dogsledders, and ice skaters in the snowy Canadian Rockies. Eagles, bobcats, wolves, bears, deer, bison, and herds of reindeer were all filmed in their natural settings. Cities and towns are part of the film, too. You can also see covered bridges, sailing ships, and even the Royal Canadian Mounted Police.

"The movie is pretty and there are many beautiful scenes," says Nita. "But I don't like standing up. They need seats in that theater!"

Ashley likes how much she learned about Canada. "I like the music and I like all the information the movie gives you about Canada," she says. "The winter scenes are my favorites."

Karyn agrees with Ashley. "All the mountains and sledding scenes are beautiful."

The Circle-Vision 360 technique makes you feel like you're actually part of the movie. David explains, "I think it's neat how Circle-Vision makes you feel like you're moving. Plus the movie shows a lot of the culture of Canada, and I like seeing all the different buildings and the rivers."

Brian agrees. "I like how they make you feel like you're moving," he says. "I think it's great—I like every part of the film."

Lissy thinks the movie has a few boring spots, but "they explain Canada well. There should be more moving sensations, though."

Don't go to this movie if you're very tired. You have to stand for the whole film.

81

UNITED KINGDOM

From London to the English countryside, this pavilion gives a varied view of the United Kingdom. Some details worth looking for include the smoke stains painted on the chimneys to make them look old and the thatched roofs that are really made of plastic broom bristles. And Tate points out, "If you like flowers, there are pretty gardens here." There's not much to do but look in the shops. Lindsay likes "looking at the different stores from the outside." Also, a group of comedians often performs along World Showcase Promenade near this pavilion.

FRANCE

The Eiffel Tower is the most recognizable landmark at the France pavilion. But it's not as tall as it seems. The same technique that makes Cinderella Castle appear taller than it is—forced perspective—is used here to make the Eiffel Tower seem to loom over Paris. The buildings are designed to look just like those you would see in a French town. Many of the people who work at the pavilion are French and speak English with a French accent.

The main attraction at the France pavilion—aside from the delicious treats at the bakery—is *Impressions de France* (Impressions of France), an

> " This movie makes me want to go to France. "
>
> —Taran (age 9)

18-minute movie that takes you from one end of France to the other. The movie is shown on a 200-degree screen, so you get to sit down and take in all the beautiful views. There are village scenes with flower markets, pastry shops, and lovely homes. There are shots of the real Eiffel Tower, the Palace of Versailles, the French countryside, wine and Champagne vineyards, the Alps, the French Riviera, and much more. Even though it's not a Circle-Vision 360 movie, it really feels as if you're moving—especially the skiing in the Alps scene. The music is the perfect soundtrack for the movie. Most of it is by French composers.

"This movie makes me want to go to France," says Taran, "especially for the skiing." Anna agrees. "Now I'd like to go see all those places. I also love the music," she says.

Karyn has been to France, and she recognizes many of the places. "It's very interesting to me because I've been to a lot of parts of France. I think it's more fun if you know what you're looking at."

Ashley is less enthusiastic. "It doesn't give enough information about France." Danielle thinks "they should explain more. But I do like the pictures they show, because France is a beautiful place."

But Lissy thinks "the pictures describe themselves. I also like when you feel like you're moving," she says. Brad especially likes "the flying parts. It feels like you're really there."

Robert says, "This is my favorite of the movies at Epcot. I like that you can sit down and rest your legs." Brian thinks the "music is great, and I like the skiing and what they show of the country." Lindsay sums it up: "This movie has colorful pictures and is a great way to learn about France."

MOROCCO

Nine tons of handmade tile were shipped to Epcot to build the Moroccan pavilion. Moroccan artists also were brought in to make sure the mosaics or tilework

would be authentic. There are replicas of monuments from several cities, including Marrakesh and Fez. A working waterwheel takes care of the irrigation for the gardens around the pavilion. There are lots of shops selling the types of things you would find in Morocco. You can buy handcrafted rugs, baskets, brass, jewelry, or a fez and other traditional Moroccan clothing. The restaurant here has a belly dancer who entertains nightly.

JAPAN

The pagoda out front makes the Japanese pavilion easy to spot. It's modeled after a pagoda in the city of Nara. The landscaping was done according to the strict Japanese method of garden design. Notice all of the evergreen trees, which in Japan are symbols of eternal life. Some of the trees found in a traditional Japanese garden will not survive in Orlando, so similar trees were used as substitutes. A drum-playing duo, known as One World Taiko, performs on the promenade outside the pavilion. The Mitsukoshi Department Store is huge and has lots of reasonably priced souvenirs from Japan.

THE AMERICAN ADVENTURE

This pavilion is the centerpiece of World Showcase. The building was constructed with 110,000 bricks—each made by hand. The American Adventure show inside celebrates the American spirit from the earliest days right up to the present. The show is narrated by Audio-Animatronics figures of Benjamin Franklin and Mark Twain. These two figures were made recently with the latest technology, so it's hard to tell they aren't real.

The show pays tribute to many of the heroes of our country: the Pilgrims, Alexander Graham Bell, history yet, we don't understand every scene." Brad agrees. "I don't understand a lot of it, but the people look so real. It's neat to see all the historic figures."

Adam says, "The characters are so realistic. I like how they walk and all the detail on their faces." Tate thinks the show is "very descriptive and very real."

Justin wasn't sure at first if the

> " It's neat to see all the historic figures. "
>
> —Brad (age 10)

Charles Lindbergh, Jackie Robinson, Walt Disney, and many more. Historic events are shown on large screens behind the characters. The show was recently updated to include events that have taken place during the last ten years.

The kids enjoy this show but think it needs more narration. Dawna says, "It's great, but for kids who haven't studied a lot of

characters are actors or Audio-Animatronics. "I was confused. I couldn't tell if they're real."

Anna thinks this show is "the perfect way to learn about our heritage. The best part is the movie at the end, which reviews all the famous Americans."

ITALY

Venice, the Italian city known for its canals, is the inspiration for this pavilion. The tower is a smaller version of the Campanile in Venice. The main building was designed to look just like the Doge's Palace. Be sure to notice the gondolas tied to the moorings in World Showcase Lagoon.

A lively group puts on very funny shows such as "The Great Impasta." An open-air market has tasty Italian chocolates and other goodies for sale. The specialty at the restaurant here is fettucine Alfredo. The waiters and waitresses sing, which Anna says "really adds to the atmosphere. It feels like you're in Italy."

GERMANY

There isn't a village in Germany quite like the one at Epcot. Instead, it's a combination of cities and small towns from all around the country. They are blended together to offer a German flavor. Try to stop by for a visit at the top of any hour so you can see and hear the specially designed glockenspiel chime.

Danielle says, "The buildings in Germany look authentic. In the center is a beautiful statue on top of a waterfall. I also like the cobblestone pavement." Tate suggests you "try the soft pretzels sold here. There's not much else to do, but it's cool to see how the buildings look in Germany."

CHINA

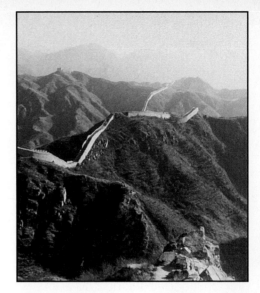

At the center of this pavilion is the Disney version of the Temple of Heaven, a landmark in the Chinese city of Beijing. Entertainers show off traditional Chinese dances with masks and streamers, and music adds to the overall atmosphere.

Inside the Temple of Heaven is another Circle-Vision 360 movie called *Wonders of China: Land of Beauty, Land of Time*. Before going in to see the movie, take a look at the waiting area. It's decorated in red and gold, and features exhibits on Chinese art and culture. When we were there, the exhibit was all about dragons. It will probably be different for your visit.

Wonders of China is a stand-up movie like *O Canada!* The 19-minute film shows a view of China that most people—kids and grown-ups—have never seen. The Chinese cities and countryside, its people, and all their ancient traditions are depicted. It's a beautiful movie, but one that's appreciated more by adults and by kids who have studied China.

"I think it's pretty interesting, but that's because I just finished studying China a few weeks ago in school," says Nita.

Karyn prefers the waiting area. "The exhibit is cool and the marble benches are pretty," she says. "I think the movie is boring. I'm not really that interested in China."

Robert, who knows a lot about dragons, likes the waiting area. "The dragon stuff is really cool. They have some neat things in there, and since I love dragons, this was my favorite part," he says. "I think the movie is boring."

Most of the kids agree that the movie is better for their parents and other adults. "It's really boring—a complete yawn," says David. Lissy agrees. "I just don't think it's very interesting," she says.

> **"The dragon stuff is really cool."**
> **—Robert (age 8)**

NORWAY

The history, folklore, and culture of one of the world's oldest countries are the focus of this pavilion. The central building is a Norwegian castle, modeled after an ancient fortress that still stands in the capital city of Oslo. Inside is the Maelstrom ride through Norwegian history. You board dragon-headed Viking boats like the one that Eric the Red sailed in.

The ride begins in a Viking village, where a ship is being built to go out to sea. The next scene takes place in the forest, where a three-headed troll curses the boat and causes it to start backing up. You are heading for a waterfall and the boat seems as if it will go over backwards. Then, just in time, it moves forward again. The ride has a few more unexpected dips and turns, and there are lightning flashes and other special effects.

"At first you think you're going down the waterfall backward."
—Brad (age 10)

After leaving the boat, you see a movie about Norway that helps explain some of the history and folklore you see on the boat ride.

Dawna says, "I like how we sit in a boat just like the ones from Norway." Brad likes how "at first you think you're going down the waterfall backward." Lindsay agrees. "It's really unpredictable. You think you're going to drop, and then you get turned back."

The kids agree that the scenery is confusing if you don't know much about Norway. "I think the movie should be first so you'll know what you're looking at on the ride," says Karyn. But Danielle has read a book about the legends of Norway, "so it's really interesting when you see them," she says. Tate adds, "The video we saw was very entertaining while it taught us about their history."

David wishes the ride was longer. "But I still think it's the best thing in World Showcase, even though it's short."

PICTURE
YOURSELF
HERE

with Mexican crafts, sombreros, and colorful blankets.

Brad thinks "the boat ride is neat. There are so many things to see." Anna agrees. "It's a good thing the boat goes slowly, so you can see all the neat scenes and Mexican figurines," she says. "I like how they have all the rocks and the atmosphere of different parts of Mexico."

For Dawna, the Mexican art is the most interesting part. "I like all the paintings, because I think Mexican art is really neat." Adam agrees. "I love all the detail of the paintings," he says. Tate thinks "the ride shows the beauty of the country."

MEXICO

The pyramid-shaped building at the Mexico pavilion is home to El Rió del Tiempo: The River of Time. This is a slow boat trip through scenes of Mexican life. You see Mexico in past centuries as well as in modern times. Film clips show cliff divers in Acapulco, speed boats in Manzanillo, and beautiful sea creatures in Isla Mujeres. There are many colorful displays depicting Mexican traditions. At the end of the boat ride, you can visit several shops

"The ride shows the beauty of the country."
—Tate (age 13)

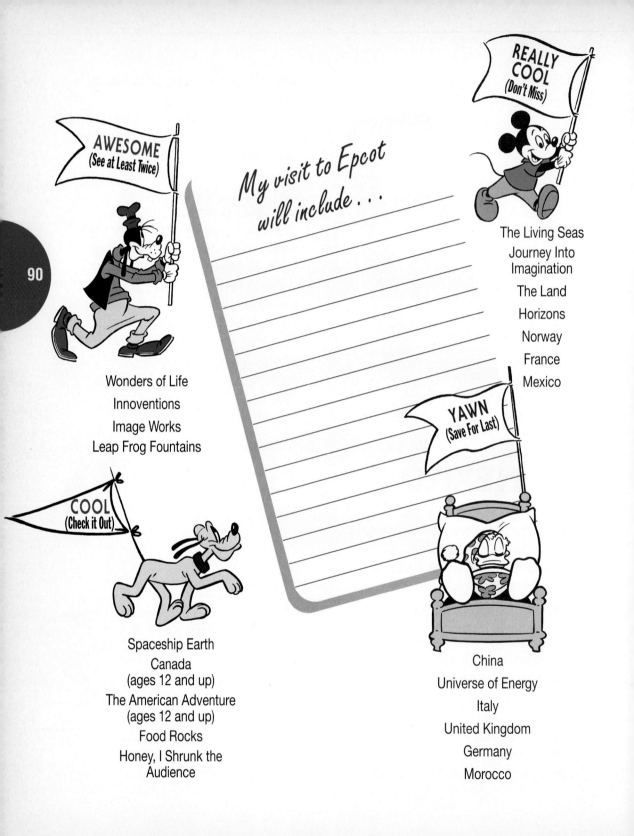

REALLY COOL
(Don't Miss)

The Living Seas
Journey Into Imagination
The Land
Horizons
Norway
France
Mexico

AWESOME
(See at Least Twice)

Wonders of Life
Innoventions
Image Works
Leap Frog Fountains

My visit to Epcot will include . . .

YAWN
(Save For Last)

China
Universe of Energy
Italy
United Kingdom
Germany
Morocco

COOL
(Check it Out)

Spaceship Earth
Canada
(ages 12 and up)
The American Adventure
(ages 12 and up)
Food Rocks
Honey, I Shrunk the Audience

Disney-MGM Studios

The Disney-MGM Studios lets you see some of the magic of making movies and television programs. There are attractions that take you behind the scenes to see how animated movies are made, how sound effects are created and edited into movies, how special effects are done, and how stunts are performed.

Other attractions include a great 3-D movie starring the Muppets, a rough ride through space on a flight simulator, a show where you can star in famous television scenes, a show that takes you "Under the Sea" with The Little Mermaid, and the newest show, The Spirit of Pocahontas.

One of the best things about the Studios is that you can participate in a number of attractions. It's fun to be right in the action, so be sure to volunteer.

It's also interesting to realize that movies and television shows are actually filmed here. During your visit, you may get a peek at people working on the next Disney animated movie, or get to see a movie or television show in the making. Some attractions open late morning and showtimes vary. Pick up an entertainment schedule so you can plan your tour around the park without wasting any time.

The Twilight Zone Tower of Terror

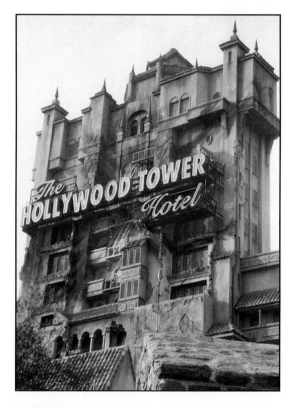

Tower of Terror is the tallest attraction at Walt Disney World. For some kids, it's also the scariest. Disney Imagineers say that Tower of Terror has a "scream factor" of 5. That means most guests scream five times on this ride! You must be at least 40 inches tall to ride.

Legend says that lightning once struck this old, run-down hotel. When you look at it from the front, you can see the part that came off. As you wait in line, you walk through different rooms, including the lobby, the library, and the boiler room. Everything is exactly as it was the night of the storm. "When lightning struck, everything just stopped," Tate explains. "You can see where the people were. There's a glass with lipstick on it, a card game that was going on, and somebody's belongings are at the front desk."

You'll have plenty of time to look around if the line is long. But as Dawna points out, "waiting just makes the suspense worse." Try to visit first thing in the morning before it gets too crowded.

The ride itself is an elevator where you're seated and strapped in. Before you get on, you have one last chance to change your mind. If you decide this ride's not for you, there's another elevator that will take you to the exit. Just remember: Once you get on the ride elevator, you can't get off.

Most of the kids were nervous, even Tate, who thinks it's scarier after you've been on a couple of times. Lindsay offers a warning: "Younger kids should know that about half the ride is in the dark." Justin says, "Some kids are scared, but I'm not."

The ride takes you on a mini-tour of the hotel, where you see many high-tech special effects. Lindsay says, "I particularly like the ghosts of the people who disappeared."

Then there's a series of drops leading to the big one. The first drop is about eight stories. The elevator shoots back up quickly and you end up on the 13th floor of the hotel. One short drop follows, with lots of sound effects that make you think the cables are breaking. Finally, you take the big plunge of 13 stories.

The kids all agree that the ride is scary. Lindsay says, "It sounds kind of freaky, but it's a thrilling experience. I was flying out of my seat!"

Dawna agrees. "This ride has to be one of the scariest at Walt Disney World. We kept going up

Say "cheese" when the elevator stops at an open window. Your picture's being taken.

and up, and then the doors opened. At the top you could see outside. You feel terrified before even falling. I was screaming all the way down."

For Karen, "The only scary thing was the drop. As soon as I got off, I thought it was really good. But then I didn't feel so well. You should definitely not go on this if you have a weak stomach."

The drops are programmed by a computer, so they can be changed to be even more exciting. It may be different during your visit, or even the next time you go on. That's good news for Dawna, who "would definitely go on again." Tate agrees. "Everyone should go on at least once," he says.

"I was screaming all the way down."

—Dawna (age 11)

Indiana Jones Epic Stunt Spectacular

ire, explosions, daring escapes, and other special effects are demonstrated at this highly rated attraction. Stunt men and women perform scenes from the movie *Raiders of the Lost Ark* and show how special effects are created. The audience watches from a large amphitheater, and several members are chosen (though no children are allowed) to perform with the pros.

"I love this show. I think it's great for all ages," says Karyn. Ashley agrees, "I think it's really neat how they do all the special effects, and how the fire blows up and how the tumblers tumble off the roofs."

One of the best parts of the

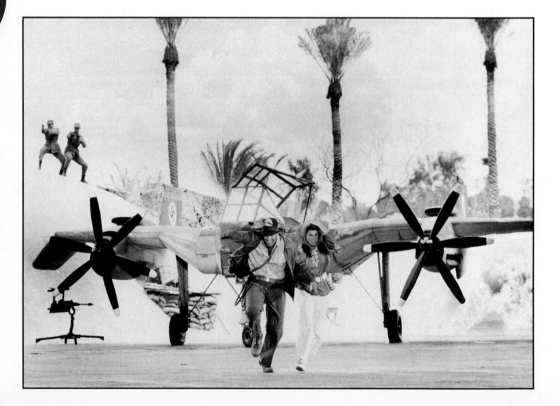

show, according to all the kids, is the scene where the giant ball rolls down and seems to crush Indiana Jones. "I was at the edge of my seat!" says Brian. Robert is amazed at the size of the ball. "The ball seems really heavy, so it would be so hard to get run over and stay alive," he says.

The kids also love the stunt men and women, and how they show us that dangerous movie stunts can be performed safely. "I love how they were falling from the towers, and then they were always okay—it's really neat," says Brian.

Lissy says the music adds to the suspense and "the stunt people are just fantastic." Brian views it as pure excitement, "especially when three of them were jumping off the trampoline and one landed in a really neat roll."

Not just entertaining, this is a show where you can learn a lot about movie stunts. "They really explain everything they're doing, making it even more fun to watch," says Karyn. David was on his feet the whole time. "It's fascinating seeing how they can get away with tricks like that," he says, "like how the guy went underground when we thought he was being chomped up by the fan."

Nita sums it up this way: "It's a show you can see many times and never get tired of it."

"I was at the edge of my seat!"

—Brian (age 12)

95

Star Tours

Soar into space on board an out-of-control StarSpeeder from the movie *Star Wars*. The flight is piloted by a new recruit, Captain Rex, who can't seem to find his way through giant ice crystals and other spaceships.

This ride takes place on a flight simulator, the same type of device used to train astronauts and pilots. The combination of the simulator and the movie on the screen makes you feel like you're really rocketing through space.

Brad says, "The pilot makes the ride really fun. He keeps going the wrong way." Robert thinks, "It's really neat. It's funny when the pilot can't find the brakes," he says. "If you know what the movie *Star Wars* is like, you'll really like this ride."

Danielle agrees. "It feels and looks like you're really

Try to go to Star Tours first thing in the morning, but not right after breakfast.

traveling through space." Dawna adds, "It feels like you're going really fast even though you're not going anywhere." Anna likes "how the seats move right to left, but the movie makes you feel like you're moving forward."

Some of the kids had been on Star Tours several times before. For them, this time wasn't as much fun. "After you go on it about ten times, it gets a little boring and seems short. But if you've never done it, it's a must," according to David. Ashley was on Star Tours for the second time. "It wasn't as much fun as the first," she says, "but I still like to get bumped around."

An experienced rider who's been on Star Tours about 15 times, Nita offers this advice: "If you're a person who likes a really rough ride, try to sit in the back."

Dawna would still "go on it again and again. It's one of the best rides at Walt Disney World."

Jim Henson's Muppet*Vision 3-D

This is one of Walt Disney World's best attractions. It begins with a very funny pre-show starring Fozzie Bear, Gonzo, Scooter, and Sam Eagle. Then you go into a specially designed theater. You see incredible 3-D effects mixed with some live special effects—so it's hard to tell what's part of the movie and what's real. Most kids can't help reaching out at least once.

"The characters come right out at you," observes Lissy. "It's really cool that they have real things happening, so when they throw the pie you think it will be a real pie, too." Adam agrees. "My favorite parts are the squirting water and when the screen blows up, because it really happens. You feel like you're going to get hit."

The real bubbles are a great special effect. "You couldn't tell which were real and which were part of the movie," says Brian. "It's really more like 4-D." Justin was also fooled by the special effect. "When I tried to touch one of them, my hand reached right through."

Taran agrees. "The whole movie is in your face!" he says. "It's awesome. I also love the little 3-D spirit, Waldo, because he seems like he's talking only to you."

Robert and Anna feel the same way. "I thought the 3-D guy was just pointing at me. I can't believe he was pointing at everyone," says Robert. And Anna says, "Waldo looks like he's always right in front of you."

"The whole movie is in your face!"

—Taran (age 9)

Nita, Karyn, and Tate have seen this attraction before. Nita reminds you to look at the back of the theater from time to time "because there's a lot of stuff happening back there and most people miss it, at least on their first visit." Tate adds, "You can really enjoy it more than once."

Karyn says, "I just love this movie. You have to see it a few times to get all the jokes and appreciate more of the details, like the two guys sitting in the balcony. They're really funny."

SuperStar Television

his is your chance to star in a famous television show. Before going inside the SuperStar Television theater, members of the audience are chosen to appear in scenes from shows such as "I Love Lucy," "Cheers," and "Home Improvement," or to hit a grand slam for the New York Mets. There are a lot of people chosen, but they don't pick too many kids. If you think you'd like to be a star, be sure to stand in the front and wave and make lots of noise.

Once inside, the people picked from the audience act out scenes and their pictures are blended with the real programs. Don't worry if you're camera shy or don't get picked. Watching is just as much fun as being on screen.

"I think it's cool that they let you participate, but you don't have to if you don't want to," says Lissy.

Karyn was chosen to be a New York Mets baseball player. "I really liked being in it, but I wish I could have seen it, too," she says. Karyn got to hit a homerun and then be

HOT TIP:

Make sure you stand in the front if you want to get picked for a part.

'I Love Lucy' scene with the chocolates on the conveyor belt. It's fun to see people from the audience play the roles of famous actors," says Brian.

"You can see it over and over again," says Nita, "because the scenes are different depending on who gets picked. It can be really funny when people goof up."

Taran's favorite part "is the David Letterman scene when he drops things off the Empire State Building." David says, "The show is neat. I like how they have the characters in just the right parts so it looks real."

interviewed by Howard Cosell. The rest of the kids enjoyed watching. "My favorite is the

101

" I really liked being in it, but I wish I could have seen it, too. "

—Karyn (age 13)

The Magic of Disney Animation

See how *Beauty and the Beast*, *Aladdin*, *The Lion King*, *Pocahontas*, and all the other Disney animated movies were created. And watch cartoon artists at work on future Disney hits, such as *The Hunchback of Notre Dame*

or *The Legend of Mulan*.

In the waiting area of this attraction, there are displays of "cels" from famous movies. (A cel is the actual painted film used in the animated movie.) There also are cels from movies that the animators are in the process of creating.

When it's time for the show, you go into a theater to see a very funny movie starring Robin Williams and Walter Cronkite. Robin is turned into a cartoon to teach us how animated films are made. After the movie, you can walk through the animation studio and see artists at work. To find out more about what they're doing, just look at the screens overhead. Robin Williams and Walter Cronkite star again. This time they're explaining each step of the animation process. Try to see this

"It's fun but you can learn at the same time."

—Lissy (age 11)

show during the day when the animators are busy working. They usually go home at about 5 P.M.

All the kids like the way this attraction makes learning fun. "I think Robin Williams is so funny," says Lissy. "It's fun but you can learn at the same time." Ashley agrees. "I like how they have Robin Williams as the character," she says. "And I like how much you learn about animation."

This attraction is especially interesting to Brian, who has taken a class in cartoon drawing. "You can learn a lot by watching, and the movie is so funny," he says. "I like how you can see real cels."

David finds it "fascinating to see all the cels that they really use in the movies. I love that you can walk through and see real animators at work. It's like taking your own personal tour."

Nita also likes the walking part of the tour the best. "It's so interesting just watching the artists work," she says.

Karyn likes that they take you step-by-step through the animation process. "It's just so neat to see how they make animated movies," she says.

"It's just so neat to see how they make animated movies."

—Karyn (age 13)

Honey, I Shrunk the Kids Movie Set Adventure

"This playground would never get boring for me."

—Robert (age 8)

The backyard in this popular movie has been re-created as an oversize playground. Even grown-ups feel small here. There are 30-foot-tall blades of grass, giant tree stumps, huge Lego toys, a big garden hose with a leak, and lots more. You have many places to explore and plenty of things to climb up and slide down.

"It looks more like honey, I blew up the garden! " says Taran. "I like the cave the best, but I advise you to take a friend because it's more fun with more people."

Robert likes it "because there are so many different places to go. This playground would never get boring for me."

Lissy thinks "the whole place is neat. Not just the slides and the swings—there's a lot for older kids to notice, like all the things that look like they come straight from the movie."

Most of the kids enjoy trying to get wet under the giant, leaky hose. This is a real challenge since water squirts from a different spot each time.

Some of the older kids prefer watching the younger kids in action. "I like the slides and the big net, but I think it's more for younger kids," says Brian.

Karyn agrees. "I'm the type of person who would just love to take a little kid around and watch them have fun."

Honey, I Shrunk the Kids Movie Set Adventure Checklist

- ☐ Bee Hive
- ☐ Cheerios
- ☐ Dog's Nose
- ☐ Leaky Hose
- ☐ Roll of Film Slide
- ☐ Spider Web
- ☐ Tree Slide
- ☐ Underground Cave

The Great Movie Ride

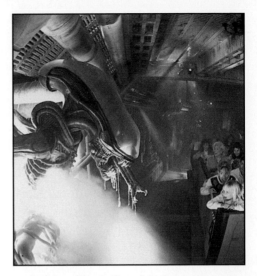

Take a ride through some of the most famous movies of all time. You pass through the sets from films including *Singin' in the Rain*, *The Wizard of Oz*, *Alien*, *Casablanca*, and *Mary Poppins*. You get caught in the middle of a shootout and come close to getting slimed by the alien. The ride ends with a movie that shows clips from great films.

"It's really cool, but it could have more action in it," says Robert. Brian thinks it's a little boring. "They tried to make it more exciting with the alien thing, but that isn't enough to make the ride really fun."

Karyn disagrees. "No matter how many times I ride, I still love it. I really love old movies, but if they want the ride to appeal to younger kids, Disney should update it so there are movies that kids know."

Ashley likes the ride just the way it is. "I think it's interesting to see all the old movies. I don't think it should be more modern."

The kids agree that the guide plays a big role in how much they like the trip. "The first time I really liked it because the guide was good," says Taran. "The second time she wasn't as good, so it was a little boring."

Lissy thinks, "The ride explains the movies really well, and the characters look almost real. I like the songs, too."

"**It's interesting to see all the old movies.**"

—Ashley (age 11)

Backstage Studio Tour

There's a real working studio at the Disney-MGM Studios. This tram ride takes you through parts of the backstage area where scenes from movies and television shows are filmed. Your trip includes Catastrophe Canyon—a great special effects show demonstrating an explosion, a fire, and a flash flood. You also get to see the costume department, the lighting department, and some props from famous movies.

"You learn something the whole time while still having fun," says Lissy. "I really like Catastrophe Canyon. It shows that special effects are much safer than they look."

Robert agrees. "Catastrophe Canyon is really cool. When the explosions go off, it gets really hot. Then when the water comes down, it gets really cold. I also like the Delta plane a lot. The guide told us that the plane has been used in filming a lot of movies."

If you like getting wet, sit on the left side of the tram.

Brian thinks part of the tour is a little boring. "I love the Catastrophe Canyon part," he says, "but I'm not crazy about the rest."

Ashley enjoys touring the back streets where "seeing the houses without the backs is cool. They

"It shows that special effects are much safer than they look."

—Lissy (age 11)

only shoot the front for the shows, so that's all they build," she points out.

"It's pretty cool how you get to see the actual homes from some television shows," adds David. "I really liked seeing the Bulldog Café from the movie *Rocketeer*."

Taran is also interested in the back streets, but for a different reason. "Catastrophe Canyon is great, but I really like the movie props because I like building models," he says.

Nita has seen this attraction before. "I like this tour," she says, "but a lot depends on the guide. If you get a really good guide, the tour is much better."

Beauty and the Beast Stage Show

Belle, Gaston, Mrs. Potts, Chip, Lumiere, Cogsworth, and the Beast come to life in this musical show based on the hit movie. The show opens with "Be Our Guest." Then it backtracks to the beginning of the story, where Belle is unhappy in her small French town. Next, Belle is held captive in the Beast's castle, and later he is attacked by all the townspeople. In the finale, Belle and the Beast declare their love and the wicked spell is broken.

"I especially love when the white doves fly out at the end," says Nita. "It adds so much to the scene. I also love the costumes and, of course, the music."

Karyn also loves this show. "There are so many details, like the dancing dishes and spoons, and the costumes are so beautiful."

Some of the kids are not as enthusiastic. "I don't like that the show starts with 'Be Our Guest' so the songs aren't in the same order as in the movie," says Ashley. "I did like the costumes, though."

Robert agrees. "The songs should be in the same order as in the movie. It's confusing," he says.

"It's weird the way the songs are mixed up, but I still like the costumes and the music," says Lissy. "The singing is really good."

Taran says, "I think if you love the movie, you'll like this show, but I'm not crazy about the movie."

> **"The songs should be in the same order as in the movie."**
>
> **—Robert (age 8)**

"I love
all the
costumes
and, of
course,
the music."
—Nita (age 14)

All the kids think that the fighting scene isn't very good. "The fighting parts don't look right—not like fighting at all," says David. Nita agrees. "I don't think little kids would get it that the dancers are supposed to be fighting," she says. "And that scene is so long."

Inside the Magic Special Effects and Production Tour

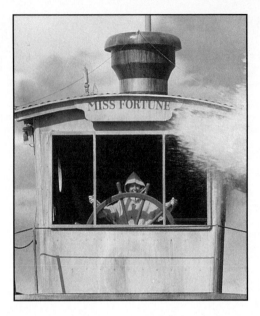

Take a behind-the-scenes look at moviemaking. On this tour, you see how some scenes from *Honey, I Shrunk the Kids* were filmed, and how a battle scene at sea is shot. You also see a short movie with Bette Midler called *The Lottery*, along with the sets where it was made. As you walk through real soundstages, you may get to see the filming of a movie or television show. The tour lasts about 40 minutes, and you walk for most of it. Be sure you have a lot of energy before starting.

The kids enjoy this attraction for different reasons. *The Lottery* was a big hit with Dawna, who at first

"thought the whole movie was filmed in New York. Then they show you all the sets here at the Studios," she says. Tate thinks "it's very interesting to see the sets and how the movies are made."

The ocean battle scene was a favorite with Justin and Brad. "I really like the bombs in the water," says Justin. Brad likes "the torpedo in the beginning. I also like that we get to see how they do special effects, and then go where they actually make the films."

Danielle finds the tour very educational. "Now when I see a movie, I'll look for the special effects." Anna says, "Learning how they make special effects in movies is educational and fun. It really keeps your interest."

> **"Learning how they make special effects in movies is educational and fun."**
>
> —Anna (age 13)

You walk for most of the tour, so be sure you have a lot of energy before starting.

The Making Of...

This movie takes an inside look at "the making of" Disney's latest animated film. You'll see the people who provide the voices of the animated stars, and the musicians whose music sets just the right mood. Some of the funniest scenes are of the animators and the wacky things they do to get into their characters.

The attraction changes to keep up with the latest Disney films. Depending on when you go, you might see *The Making of Pocahontas*, *The Making of Toy Story*, or *The Making of The Hunchback of Notre Dame*.

Voyage of the Little Mermaid

This live show has all your favorite characters from *The Little Mermaid* acting out the story on stage. Ariel and Prince Eric are played by actors. Flounder, Sebastian, and other sea creatures are played by puppets. The puppeteers are dressed all in black, so it looks like the puppets are suspended in mid-air. A huge Ursula battles with Ariel.

There are some great special

effects that really draw you into the show. A screen of water makes you feel like you're under the sea. There are lasers, lightning, and a mist that sprays into the audience. There also are clips from the movie shown on a screen on stage. Several songs are performed to tell the story.

Dawna thinks "the combination of live actors, puppets, movie clips, lasers, bubbles, and water all add up to a great show."

Adam says, "I really like the lasers, and how they make it look like you're under water." Lindsay agrees. "This is a totally creative show. You feel like you're under the water, especially when you get wet with the mist."

Justin was surprised by the show. "I don't really like *The Little Mermaid*, so I thought it would be stupid. But it ends up being really good," he says.

Tate thinks they leave out too much. "I would like to see a few more scenes added to fill out the story," he says. "Even though most people know what happens, it would be better to have more scenes."

"This is a totally creative show."

—Lindsay (age 9)

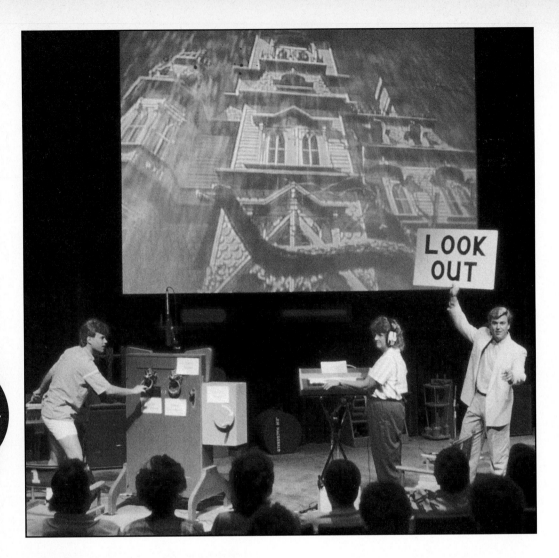

LOOK OUT

Monster Sound Show

Don't be fooled by the name of the Monster Sound Show. There are no monsters in this show. Instead, audience members are chosen to help create sound effects for a movie. One person is in charge of the doorknocker, someone else takes care of the crashing chandelier, another creates the sound of thunder. Other sound effects include footsteps, a creaking door, wind, and a groaning man.

The short movie, starring Chevy Chase and Martin Short, is shown once with professional sound effects. Then audience members try to fill in and copy the effects when the movie is shown again. The film is shown once more with the new effects. They usually don't match very well, but that's part of the fun.

"It's great to see how some of the sounds in movies are made. There are a lot of mess-ups, and that's really funny," says Lindsay. Adam agrees. "It's really neat how they can record sound effects and put them into the movie," he says.

Anna thinks it's fun for the volunteers and for the audience. "The people up on the stage must have the time of their lives, and the audience has a pretty good time, too."

Brad likes the last playback of the movie. "It's cool. When the sounds are supposed to happen there's nothing, and then later you hear the wrong sound," he says.

After the movie, go to the area called SoundWorks, where you can have some hands-on sound effects experiences. "The 3-D room is really fun," says Tate. "Everything sounds like it's actually happening to you." Danielle agrees. "You feel like the people are in the room with you," she says. "You can even hear the guy getting his haircut."

"**It's really neat how they can record sound effects and put them into the movie.**"

—Adam (age 14)

The Spirit of Pocahontas Stage Show

This new stage show celebrates the legend and lessons of Pocahontas, the heroine of Walt Disney's 33rd animated film. With the explorer John Smith, this young Native American woman proves that peace is possible—even among people as different as the Powhatan Indians and the English settlers.

Like the *Pocahontas* movie, the stage show highlights the beauty of the outdoors. The show wasn't open when we visited, but here's an idea of what to expect.

You enter the theater, surrounded by the sounds of the woodland. Leaves are rustling, water is flowing, and animals are calling to one another. A drumbeat begins and the curtain is flung open on the scene of a Powhatan ceremonial fire. Dancers appear and, in a puff of smoke, you see Kekata, the medicine man and narrator. He welcomes you and invites you to hear the tale of "one special spirit…The Spirit of Pocahontas." The story is told through dance and song, costumes, masks, giant puppets, and other props.

Pocahontas is a free spirit who can travel wherever the wind takes her. With the help of special effects, she appears and disappears throughout the show. You see her in the enchanted glade where she seeks the wisdom of Grandmother Willow. Later, she's on the branch of a tree, spying on John Smith. When he spots her, she comes down to meet him and they fall in love.

If you've seen the movie, you know of the clash between the

Don't miss this exciting new stage show.

other settlers and the Powhatan tribe. And you know that the war is stopped because of Pocahontas and John Smith.

The high point of the show comes in the middle of the fighting scene. John Smith is knocked to the ground and is about to meet his death. All of a sudden there's a clap of thunder and Pocahontas appears. "Look around you," she says. "This is where the path of hatred has brought you." Then John Smith and Pocahontas disappear. In their place is the Medicine Man who points out the lesson of Pocahontas: hatred is a spirit for us all to fear.

PICTURE
YOURSELF
HERE

PICTURE
YOURSELF
HERE

AWESOME
(See at Least Twice)

Jim Henson's
Muppet*Vision 3-D

Star Tours

Indiana Jones Epic
Stunt Spectacular

Tower of Terror

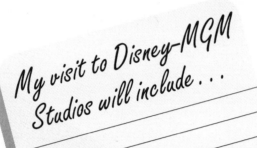

*My visit to Disney-MGM
Studios will include . . .*

REALLY COOL
(Don't Miss)

The Magic of Disney
Animation

SuperStar Television

Special Effects and
Production Tour

Monster Sound
Show

Voyage of the
Little Mermaid

The Spirit of
Pocahontas
Stage Show

COOL
(Check it Out)

Beauty and the Beast
Stage Show

The Great Movie Ride

Backstage Studio Tour

Honey, I Shrunk the Kids
Movie Set Adventure

YAWN
(Save For Last)

no yawns here!

Everything Else in the World

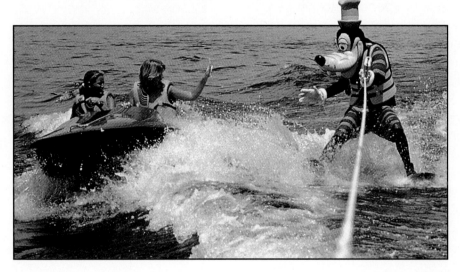

When most kids think about Walt Disney World, they think of the Magic Kingdom, Epcot, and Disney-MGM Studios. But as we discovered on our trips, there's much more to see.

There's a petting farm filled with baby animals, a wooded campground with a water park known as River Country, an island where endangered species are cared for, two state-of-the-art water parks called Typhoon Lagoon and Blizzard Beach, lakes where you can rent boats, the Disney Village Marketplace, a behind-the-scenes program called Wonders of Walt Disney World, and lots of restaurants and hotels.

In this chapter you can read about all these extras and decide which ones you most want to see. The kids agree that making time for Discovery Island and renting Water Sprites for a ride on one of Walt Disney World's waterways are a great break from the theme park routine.

So read on and help your parents decide where to stay, where to eat, and which added attractions to visit.

DISCOVERY ISLAND

Discovery Island is the perfect place to spend a morning—or even a whole day—away from the theme parks. You can see many different types of birds, huge turtles, and several endangered species. It's like a natural zoo with lots of trees and plants, so you feel almost like you're in a forest. You can explore the island on your own by using the map you get when you arrive and by following the marked paths. Kids ages 8 to 14 can sign up for a Discovery Island Kidventure, a four-hour guided tour (see the box on the next page for details).

Besides looking at all the animals and plants, you can learn

" It's a place I could go to 100 times and never be bored. "

—Robert

(age 8)

"You can see animals that you would never see anywhere else."

—Lissy (age 11)

Discovery Island Kidventure

If you think you'd like to explore Discovery Island with an expert, kids ages 8 to 14 can sign up for the four-hour tour that includes transportation, lunch, crafts materials, and a souvenir photo. The cost is $32. You must make a reservation in advance. The phone number for reservations is 407-824-3784.

about different products that are bad for the environment and harmful to endangered animals. There's also a hospital right on the island where injured animals are cared for. You can look in through glass windows and see the veterinarian at work.

The kids agree that Discovery Island should definitely be on your schedule. Most of them never even knew it existed. "I'm surprised that this is at Walt Disney World," says Lissy.

Along the paths you get to see birds that sound like other animals. "I like the barking swan and the bird that sounds like a croaking frog," says Ashley. "It's neat that that's how they protect their territory."

Nita likes that "they take care of all the animals, even ones that don't belong there. The hospital is nice, too. It looks just like a real hospital," she says.

David thinks Discovery Island is a "great way to see these birds, maybe for the last time. They're

trying to save a lot of birds that are becoming extinct."

For Robert, the whole island is great. "It's a place I could go to 100 times and never be bored," he says.

The kids got to see some animals up close, like a baby alligator, a hedgehog, and the huge turtles. "The hedgehog is pretty cute," says Ashley, "and the turtles are neat but they smell bad."

Lissy says, "You can see animals that you would never see anywhere else. It's so exotic. The place is just awesome."

121

FORT WILDERNESS

Tucked away in a wooded area of Walt Disney World is Fort Wilderness. There are many activities here, and some people actually stay in trailers in the woods. You can bring your own trailer from home or you can rent a trailer furnished like a hotel room. There are a few pools, tennis courts, volleyball courts, hayrides, a huge marina with lots of boats, and a petting farm. River Country water park also is located here. It's described later in this chapter on page 128.

Fort Wilderness has so much to offer, you could spend days here without seeing everything. If you only have a couple of hours, explore the petting farm and rent Water Sprites for a ride around Bay Lake.

Fort Wilderness Petting Farm

This small farm is home to some extra-friendly goats, several sheep, a donkey, rabbits, pigs, chickens, and a few other birds and animals, including ponies that you can ride.

The kids agree that the farm is great for younger children and fun for kids their own age, too. "The farm gives you a chance to get up close to the animals without being afraid of anything," says Lissy. Robert agrees. "I especially like letting the little baby goats chew on my fingers," he says.

Karyn remembers that she "used to love petting farms. But now it's a little boring. If you really like

Water Sprites

These small motor boats don't actually go very fast, but they feel like they do. With the wind whipping in your face and the nose of the boat lifting into the air, the sensation of speed is great. You must be at least 12 years old to drive a Water Sprite everywhere but at the Disney Village Marketplace, where you have to be 14 years old (with or without an adult). If you're under that age, you can ride as a passenger with a parent or an older brother or sister. The younger kids in our group rode with the older kids instead of with an adult.

The Water Sprite trip gets very high marks from all the kids. The rental is for 30 minutes, and you can cover a lot of Bay Lake in that time. You can even make a trip around Discovery Island. Water Sprites can be rented at some other locations. See the end of this section for details.

"It's awesome," says Brian. "I was turning into the waves and one splashed on top of me."

David thinks being able to drive your own boat is neat. "I love going over the water," he says. "This is fun at Fort Wilderness that you definitely can't miss." Lissy thinks the Water Sprites are "loads

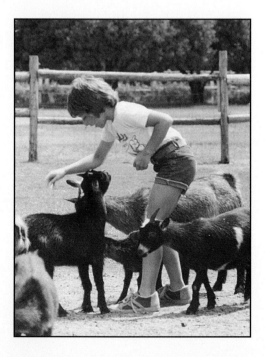

animals, though, you'd have fun no matter how old you are." Brian agrees. "I recommend this place for anyone who loves animals," he says.

Where to Rent Water Sprites

Water Sprites can also be rented at the Contemporary Resort, the Polynesian Resort, the Grand Floridian Resort, the Wilderness Lodge Resort, the Caribbean Beach Resort, and the Disney Village Marketplace. The cost is $12 for a half-hour. You must be 12 years old to drive, except at the Disney Village Marketplace, where you must be 14 years old.

of fun, and being in the water really cools you off."

Karyn likes the scenery around the lake. "It's fun to go all around Discovery Island because it's really pretty with all the trees."

Some of the kids think the boats should go faster, but Nita says, "It's not too fast and not too slow."

More Fun at Fort Wilderness

There are many other activities available at Fort Wilderness. You can rent a canoe ($4 per hour or $10 per day) for a trip along the canals around the campground. Or you can rent a bicycle ($3 per hour or $8 per day) and explore one of the many trails. At the Horse Barn, you can see the champion Percherons that pull the trolleys down Main Street in the Magic Kingdom. Sometimes the blacksmith is there to answer questions about the special shoes he makes for the horses. There are hayrides that last about an hour and cost $4 for kids (ages 3 to 11) and $6 for adults. It's also possible to go on an organized fishing trip, or just to fish in the canals.

WATERS OF THE WORLD

Walt Disney World is a water wonderland. With three spectacular water parks and the unique swimming pools at the resorts, getting wet, staying cool, and having fun at Walt Disney World is very easy. If you want to go swimming, try to avoid January and February. Even Florida weather can be cool during these months. Here's a description of the water parks and some of the special pools so you can decide which you'd like to try out most.

Typhoon Lagoon

This watery playground is a great place to spend a whole day. The surf lagoon is larger than two football fields, and the 4½-foot waves make body surfing fun. There are two speed slides that send you through a cave at 30 miles per hour, a couple of winding storm slides, and a whitewater slide that gives groups

Arrive at Typhoon Lagoon or Blizzard Beach as soon as they open or wait until late afternoon.

and families a chance to ride the rapids together. There's also a special area just for younger children called Ketchakiddie Creek, which has smaller slides and other games.

On top of Mount Mayday, the mountain in the center of Typhoon Lagoon, there's a boat called the *Miss Tilly*. Keep an eye on the smokestack on top of the boat. It shoots a flume of water every 30 minutes. If you climb to the top of Mount Mayday, you get a great view of all the activities at Typhoon Lagoon.

The biggest water slides are two speed slides called Humunga Cowabunga. Castaway Creek is a stream that circles the entire park. You can hop in an oversize tube and float around Castaway Creek. There are lots of props along the way, and you can get in and out of the creek at many locations.

There's also a volleyball court, a shop, two restaurants, and lots of lounge chairs for your parents.

Blizzard Beach

The newest water park at Walt Disney World also offers the most thrills. Blizzard Beach opened in the spring of 1995 with some of the longest, fastest slides. It also has plenty of activities for those who like less excitement, so there should be something here for everyone in your family.

We got an advance look at Blizzard Beach during our trip. "This is one awesome water park," says Karyn. "Everything is so detailed and exciting."

Blizzard Beach was designed to look like an Olympic ski resort. And like a ski resort, everything centers around the mountain—in this case, the 90-foot-high Mt. Gushmore. On top of the mountain is an observation tower that gives you a view of the park and all the action below. Or, get a closer look on Cross Country Creek, a raft ride that slowly circles the entire park.

The biggest thrill at Blizzard Beach is Summit Plummet. This ride begins 120 feet in the air, on a platform that looks just like a ski jump. It sends you down a 500-foot slide at about 55 miles per hour. That's as fast as most cars on the highway.

Slush Gusher is a speed slide that also takes you down Mt. Gushmore, but not quite as fast. Other activities—including tube slides, boat rides, water slide races, and inner tube rides—keep you busy all day long. When you're ready to relax, try the free-form pool. Its gentle waves make it great for swimming or just hanging out.

For preteens, there's Ski Patrol Training Center featuring a slide, an "iceberg" obstacle course, and ropes for swinging over and into the water. For younger kids, there's Tike's Peak, with a smaller version of Mt. Gushmore's slides and a snow castle fountain play area.

River Country

If you've ever read *The Adventures of Tom Sawyer* and *The Adventures of Huckleberry Finn*, River Country will seem like it came right from those stories. Disney Imagineers have created a swimming hole just like the ones Tom and Huck used to visit—only this one is much bigger. It has a huge swimming pool with two steep water slides. The main section of River Country is Bay Cove, an area with rope swings, a ship's boom, and other things made for swinging and jumping into the water. Bay Cove also has two flume rides that send you down a corkscrew path into the water.

Other River Country activities include a whitewater ride in a large inner tube, an area with smaller slides and water toys for younger kids, and a small beach. There's also a snack stand.

Hotel Pools

There are some great pools at the Walt Disney World resorts. You're allowed to swim in the pools only if you're a guest of the

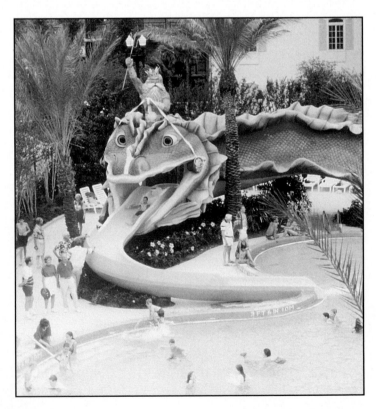

hotel. So read this section carefully, and read the rest of the hotel information later in this chapter on page 139. Then you can give your parents advice on where you'd most like to stay.

One of the best pools is Stormalong Bay at the Yacht Club and Beach Club resorts. There's a sunken ship with a built-in water slide so you can climb the wreck and slide back down to the water. At Port Orleans, Doubloon Lagoon is a pool built around a sea serpent that may still be lingering underground. His tail can be seen jutting up in spots along the walkways, and the water slide is actually the serpent's tongue. Ol' Man Island is a 3½-acre recreation center at Dixie Landings. It features a large pool with slides and ropes. At the Polynesian Resort, the Swimming Pool Lagoon is surrounded by a large cluster of boulders that actually is a water slide. The Grotto Pool between the Dolphin and Swan hotels is a group of connecting pools with bridges and a water slide. At the All-Star Sports Resort, the main pool looks like an ocean with circling sharks. At the All-Star Music Resort, one pool is in the shape of a guitar and the other is in the shape of a piano.

Where To Get Wet in the Theme Parks

There are several attractions around the three major parks that offer chances to get wet. At the Magic Kingdom, try Splash Mountain (especially if you sit in the front row). At Epcot, you can spend hours playing at the jumping fountains outside the Journey Into Imagination pavilion. At the Disney-MGM Studios, the Backstage Studio Tour provides a splash during Catastrophe Canyon (sit on the left for a wetter ride), and the leaky hoses at the Honey, I Shrunk the Kids Movie Set Adventure playground spurt water unexpectedly.

RESTAURANT GUIDE

There are so many restaurants at Walt Disney World that you should have no trouble finding someplace with food you like. To help you sort through the choices, here are our recommendations for the best eating spots for kids. Remember, this is not a complete listing of all the restaurants at Walt Disney World.

When you plan your day, look at this list and choose a restaurant near where you expect to be at mealtime. Then read through the selections to find a place that serves food you like. The key below explains the letters and dollar signs at the end of each listing. The letters tell you which meals are served. The dollar signs give you an idea of how much your meal will cost. If a restaurant has the letter "B" at the end of its listing, a full breakfast is offered there.

B reakfast
L unch
D inner
S nacks
$ Inexpensive
$$ Moderate
$$$ Expensive

MAGIC KINGDOM

Waitress Service

King Stefan's Banquet Hall: Fantasyland. Daily character breakfast. At lunch and dinner, prime ribs, beef, chicken, salads. $$$. B, L, D.

Liberty Tree Tavern: Liberty Square. Daily all-you-can-eat character dinner. Seafood, chicken, beef, sandwiches, salads. $$$. L, D.

Tony's Town Square: Main Street. Pizza, spaghetti with meatballs, Italian sandwiches. $$. B, L, D.

Fast Food

Aunt Polly's Landing: Tom Sawyer Island. Sandwiches, soft-serve ice cream, lemonade. $. L, S.

Columbia Harbour House: Liberty Square. Seafood, sandwiches, salads. $. L, D, S.

Cosmic Ray's Starlight Café: Tomorrowland. Soups, salads, burgers, sandwiches, chicken. $. L, D, S.

Crystal Palace: Main Street. Cafeteria: pasta, hot dogs, fish, chicken, salads. $$. B, L, D, S.

Diamond Horseshoe Saloon Revue: Frontierland. Western show. Sandwiches, chips. $. L, S.

Lumière's Kitchen: Fantasyland. Chicken nuggets, grilled cheese, cookies. $. L, D, S.

Pecos Bill Café: Frontierland. Burgers, barbecued chicken sandwiches, hot dogs. $. L, D, S.

Pinocchio Village Haus: Fantasyland. Burgers, hot dogs, sandwiches, salads. $. L, D, S.

Snack Spots

Auntie Gravity's Galactic Goodies: Tomorrowland. Frozen yogurt, fresh fruit. $. S.

Liberty Square Market: Liberty Square. Fresh fruit. $. S.

Plaza Ice Cream Parlor: Main Street. Lots of flavors. $. S.

Mrs. Potts' Cupboard: Fantasyland. Sundaes, floats. $. S.

Sunshine Tree Terrace: Adventureland. Orange slush, frozen yogurt shakes. $. S.

Westward Ho: Frontierland. Cookies, pretzels, chips. $. S.

Pasta Piazza Ristorante:
Innoventions. Pizza, pasta.
$. B, L, D, S.
Pure & Simple: Wonders of Life.
Sandwiches, salads, waffles,
frozen yogurt, juices. $. L, S.
Sunshine Season Food Fair: The
Land. Food court. $. L, D, S.

World Showcase

Waitress Service

Au Petit Café: France. Sautéed
chicken fingers, pasta, ground
beef steaks. $$ to $$$. L, D, S.
Biergarten: Germany. Chicken,
frankfurters, sausages, potato
pancakes. $$ to $$$. L, D.
**L'Originale Alfredo di Roma
Ristorante:** Italy. Pasta, chicken,
veal. $$$. L, D.
Marrakesh: Morocco. Chicken,
bastila (cinnamon chicken in
pastry), sampler platters. $$$. L, D.
San Angel Inn: Mexico. Chicken,
beef, guacamole, tacos. $$$. L, D.
Teppanyaki Dining Rooms:
Japan. Stir-fried meat, vegetables,
fish cooked at the table. $$$. L, D.

Fast Food

Cantina de San Angel: Mexico.
Burritos, tortillas with chicken,
tacos, nachos. $. L, D.
Kringla Bakeri og Kafe: Norway.
Sandwiches, pastries. $. L, S.

EPCOT
Future World

Waitress Service

Coral Reef: Living Seas. Seafood,
pasta, chicken. $$$. L, D.
Garden Grill: The Land. Daily
character meals. Sandwiches,
pasta, chicken, steaks, burgers.
$$ to $$$. B, L, D.

Fast Food

Electric Umbrella: Innoventions.
Burgers, chicken sandwiches,
hot dogs, salads, frozen
yogurt. $. L, D, S.

Liberty Inn: The American Adventure. Burgers, hot dogs, chicken sandwiches, fries, ice cream. $ to $$. L, D, S.

Lotus Blossom Café: China. Sweet-and-sour pork, stir-fried beef, egg rolls, soup. $. L, D.

Sommerfest: Germany. Bratwurst sandwiches, soft pretzels, apple strudel. $. L, D, S.

Yakitori House: Japan. Yakitori (skewered chicken), teriyaki sandwiches. $. L, D, S.

Snack Spots

Boulangerie Pâtisserie: France. Pastries, croissants, éclairs, chocolate mousse. $. S.

Refreshment Outpost: Between Germany and China. Frozen yogurt or ice cream. $. S.

Refreshment Port: Canada. Frozen yogurt, cookies, fruit. $. S.

Eating Healthy

Most restaurants, including fast-food stands, now have a lot more healthy foods such as salads, fresh fruit, broiled or grilled chicken breasts, turkey burgers, and nonfat frozen yogurt.

DISNEY-MGM STUDIOS
Waitress Service

50's Prime Time Café: Macaroni and cheese, burgers, tuna salad sandwiches, chicken pot pie, hot roast beef, alphabet soup, ice cream sodas, shakes. $$. L, D, S.

Mama Melrose's Ristorante Italiano: Pizza, lasagna, meatball subs, chicken, pasta. $$ to $$$. L, D (dinner only offered seasonally).

Sci-Fi Dine-In Theater: Burgers, pasta, salads. $$ to $$$. L, D.

Fast Food

Backlot Express: Chicken, burgers, hot dogs, sandwiches, salads. $. L, D, S.

Commissary: Sandwiches, burgers, salads. $. L, D.

Food Courts

Food courts make it easy to satisfy everyone in your family at mealtimes. We tried Old Port Royale at the Caribbean Beach Resort. Its six counters serve everything from pizza and pasta to burgers, sandwiches, and Chinese food. For dessert, there's a bakery that also serves ice cream. The kids like being able to choose their own meals. Brian says, "There are a lot of good things to eat. I love all the selections." Ashley agrees. "I especially like the pizza," she says.

Other hotel food courts are at Port Orleans, Dixie Landings, All-Star Sports, and All-Star Music resorts. At the theme parks, you'll find the Sunshine Season Food Fair in The Land pavilion of Epcot, and the Soundstage at the Disney-MGM Studios.

134

Hollywood & Vine: Chicken, spaghetti and meatballs, tortellini, ribs, salads. $$. B, L, D.
Soundstage: Food court with *Aladdin* and *Pocahontas* settings. Daily character breakfast. $. B, L, D.

Snack Spots
Dinosaur Gertie's: Frozen slush drinks, fruit yogurt bars, frozen bananas. $. S.
Studio Catering Co.: Fresh fruit, sundaes, milk shakes. $. S.

Eating with the Characters

Kids of all ages enjoy having breakfast with the characters—especially since it's so easy to have your picture taken with them. David thinks "seeing all the Disney characters joke and dance around makes breakfast very special." Below is a list of where you can eat with the characters. To make reservations call 407-WDW-DINE.

Contemporary Café,
  Contemporary
'Ohana, Polynesian
1900 Park Fare,
  Grand Floridian
Artist Point, Wilderness Lodge
Cape May Café, Beach Club
Harry's Safari, Dolphin
Garden Grove, Swan
Olivia's, Disney Vacation Club

You can also eat breakfast with the characters at Chef Mickey's at the Disney Village Marketplace, King Stefan's in the Magic Kingdom, Garden Grill in Epcot, and Soundstage in the Disney-MGM Studios. Dinners with the characters are held at the Grand Floridian and Swan resorts, Garden Grill in Epcot (all meals), and Liberty Tree Tavern in the Magic Kingdom.

Hot Tip: Ask about portion sizes if you don't order from the kids menu or you may get way too much food.

135

Kid Favorites

Although almost every restaurant at Walt Disney World caters to kids, our group definitely has its favorites. At the top of the list is Planet Hollywood near Pleasure Island. "If you like movies, this is the place to be," says Dawna. "The bus from *Speed* is hanging from the ceiling! Movie scenes run constantly on a big screen. And everything tastes great."

Whispering Canyon Café in the Wilderness Lodge also is a big hit. "The dinner is incredible," says Karyn. Lindsay likes "how they bring all the food out and you help yourself."

Nita recommends Chef Mickey's Village Restaurant in the Disney Village Marketplace, where you get a big selection and a chance to meet Mickey Mouse. "I would tell others about this place," she says.

For a quick bite in the Magic Kingdom, try Pecos Bill Café. Karyn says, "The Wild West setting is fun, and the food is great." Taran agrees. "My chicken sandwich was awesome, and we got the food fast," he says.

If you have more time, Tony's Town Square on Main Street is a good choice for kids and parents. Dawna says, "This is where Lady and Tramp ate. I had spaghetti and meatballs just like they did."

For fast food in Epcot, try Pasta Piazza in Future World. "The pizza is excellent, even though the pieces are a little big," says Tate. The kids also like the Liberty Inn in World Showcase. Brad says, "The food is good. There's a little more

Eating at the Hotels

Most of the Walt Disney World resorts have several restaurants. Here's our list of the best spots for kids in each hotel.

Contemporary:	Contemporary Café
Polynesian:	'Ohana
Grand Floridian:	1900 Park Fare
Wilderness Lodge:	Whispering Canyon Café
Caribbean Beach:	Old Port Royale Food Court
Yacht and Beach Club:	Beaches & Cream Soda Shop
Dolphin:	Coral Café
Swan:	Garden Grove Café
Dixie Landings:	Colonel's Cotton Mill Food Court
Port Orleans:	Sassagoula Floatworks & Food Factory
Disney Vacation Club:	Olivia's Café
All-Star Sports and Music:	End Zone and Intermission Food Courts
Fort Wilderness:	Trail's End Buffet

selection than usual."

At the Disney-MGM Studios, the Sci-Fi Dine-In Theater gets rave reviews. Dawna says, "The restaurant is set up like a drive-in movie theater. You sit in a car with a table and there are old science fiction movies showing." Anna adds, "The waitresses are even on skates."

The kids agree that the 50's Prime Time Café at the Disney-MGM Studios is one of their top choices. David says, "I've never had so much fun in a restaurant in my entire life." Lissy thinks "it's so neat how the waitresses and waiters pretend to be Mom and Dad." Nita picks this as the best choice for both parents and kids. "No matter how old you are, you can become a kid at the 50's Prime Time Café," she says.

Of course, all restaurants can't please everybody. Keep in mind the type of food you like when making your choice. That's where our Restaurant Guide can help. Here's a tip from Anna: "Pecos Bill Café is good for kids who like fast food and just want a burger."

All the kids agree that the buffet-style clambake at Cape May Café at the Beach Club Resort is a good

Dinner Shows

At the Hoop-Dee-Doo Musical Revue, a group of entertainers sings, dances, and tells jokes, while you eat a dinner of fried chicken, ribs, and corn-on-the-cob. Danielle says, "They get everyone in on the fun and put on a wonderful show." David thinks the show is "very funny. I was laughing the whole time." Tate says, "Anybody in the Orlando area should go see it. It's the perfect combination of great food and entertainment."

Other dinner shows include the Polynesian Luau and Mickey's Tropical Revue at the Polynesian Resort. The Biergarten at Epcot's Germany pavilion features a show with traditional German musicians. Reservations for these shows must be made well in advance by calling 407-WDW-DINE.

choice for lots of different tastes. Danielle likes that "they have something for everyone. There are different kinds of seafood, but also salads, pasta, and chicken." Lindsay says, "If you can't find something here, you won't find it anywhere."

Snack Wagons

All around the theme parks are wagons that sell soft drinks, popcorn, and lots of ice cream—Cookies 'n' Cream ice cream sandwiches, Mouseketeer Bars, lowfat strawberry yogurt, and strawberry bars. Some wagons offer fresh fruit, too.

WALT DISNEY WORLD RESORTS

There are 15 resorts around the Walt Disney World property. That means there are enough rooms at Walt Disney World for you to stay in a different spot every night for almost 48 years!

We visited most of the resorts during our trips. Here are brief descriptions of all the resorts at Walt Disney World. There's information on the things that are most important to kids, like gamerooms, special programs, restaurants, and fun activities. For more details about the hotel pools, see pages 128 and 129.

Near the Magic Kingdom

Contemporary: The monorail rides through the center of this modern-style hotel. There are two restaurants, two pools, a playground, boat rentals, seven shops, and a huge gameroom. "If you love to play video games, you'll love this place," says Ashley. The kids also like that the monorail travels right through the building.

Polynesian: The decor here looks like it comes straight from the South Seas, with beautiful plants and trees all around. There are three restaurants, two pools, a playground, boat rentals, a gameroom, and six shops. "The Polynesian has a beautiful beach," says Brian. Nita and David like the pool with its big slide.

Grand Floridian: At first, this elegant hotel seems to be designed for grown-ups only, but it's fun for kids, too. There's a pool, boat rentals, a playground, a gameroom, and four shops.

139

Wilderness Lodge: With its log columns and totem poles, this hotel offers a taste of the American West. "You really feel like you're in the wilderness," says Lindsay. Dawna likes that "people sit in rocking chairs just watching the fire—in Florida!" This hotel has two restaurants, a pool, bike and boat rentals, a playground, a gameroom, and a special Cubs Den program for kids.

Fort Wilderness Campground: Guests can either camp with their own equipment or rent a trailer home at this wooded campground. There are two restaurants, two pools, a large beach, boat and bicycle rentals, a petting farm, pony rides, two gamerooms, and two shops.

Near Epcot and the Studios

Caribbean Beach: The rooms at this hotel are located in many colorful buildings. There's one main pool, plus five smaller pools, a food court, boat and bicycle rentals, a playground, a small gameroom, and one shop. "It's a pretty hotel because of all the colors," says Nita.

Yacht Club and Beach Club: There are really two hotels here that connect in the center. One has a boating theme and the other has a beach theme. There's a large main pool, plus two smaller ones, five restaurants and an ice cream parlor, boat rentals, a gameroom, and two shops.

Dolphin: You can't miss the giant dolphin statues on top of this hotel. The Dolphin has six restaurants, an ice cream parlor, a gameroom, two pools, boat rentals, four shops, and Camp Dolphin, a program just for kids. "Camp Dolphin is great and the rooms are very nice," says Ashley.

Swan: The Swan and Dolphin are similar because they were designed by the same architect. The Swan has two pools, three restaurants, boat rentals, a small gameroom, Camp Swan (a children's program), and one shop.

Port Orleans: The special details at this hotel make it look like the city it's named for, New Orleans. There's one restaurant and a food court, a large specially designed pool, boat and bicycle rentals, a gameroom, and a shop.

Dixie Landings: Next door to Port Orleans, this hotel represents the countryside surrounding New Orleans. There's one restaurant and a food court, a large pool on a recreation island, plus five more pools, boat and bicycle rentals, a gameroom, and a shop.

Disney Vacation Club: The townhouses that make up this resort are more like homes. There are two restaurants, one main pool, plus smaller pools around the resort, a small gameroom, boat and bicycle rentals, and a shop.

There are VCRs in the rooms and you can see movies and other videotapes for free. Karyn thinks it "would be a nice place to stay for a while because it's so homey."

The Villas at The Disney Institute: There are several types of villas, including "treehouses" on stilts. There's one restaurant, six pools, boat and bicycle rentals, and several small gamerooms.

All-Star Resorts: Sports and music fans will want to try these two resorts. All-Star Sports has five buildings, each built around a different sport—tennis, football, surfing, baseball, and basketball. At All-Star Music the buildings are themed around five types of music—rock and roll, calypso, Broadway tunes, country and western, and jazz. Each hotel has its own food court, playground, and large arcade, plus two pools. Anna says, "This is the coolest place to stay, at least for kids." Lindsay adds, "The arcades have every game you could imagine."

141

ENTERTAINMENT

There's always entertainment going on at Walt Disney World. When you arrive in each theme park, pick up an entertainment schedule so you can decide what to see. Here are descriptions of some of the best shows.

The Magic Kingdom

SpectroMagic: This parade makes its way down Main Street twice each night during busy seasons. The advanced technology uses holograms, special lighting, and a state-of-the-art sound system to create a show that, as Dawna says, "No one should miss. It's a perfect way to end an evening or a trip." Lindsay agrees. "The dazzling lights make it gorgeous."

Mickey Mania Parade: Mickey is everywhere in this parade, held daily at 3 P.M. along Main Street. Look for him on the costumes of the paraders and on the tires of the vehicles. There are stiltwalkers, rollerbladers, BMX bikers, and characters on giant tricycles. All move to the beat of the song, "Rock the House with the Mouse."

Fantasy in the Sky Fireworks: Even those who don't like fireworks can't keep their eyes off this display. The show is presented nightly when the park is open until 10 P.M. It uses about 200 shells—all set off within five minutes to create fantastic bursts of color.

Kids of the Kingdom: This group performs often in the Castle Forecourt. Their show has lively singing and dancing to Disney tunes—plus appearances by Disney characters. Danielle says, "The dancers are great and so are the characters." Justin offers this advice: "If you don't get a chance to see a lot of the characters, then go to this show."

Epcot

IllumiNations: A spectacular laser, water, and fireworks show takes place each night at Epcot around World Showcase Lagoon. The best spot to see it is on the little island between The American Adventure and Italy. "The lights, lasers, and fireworks are really cool," says Lissy. Tate thinks "the lasers are the best part." Adam likes the spinning globe and "how the fountains go up and down."

World Showcase Kids Day Celebrations: One day each month, every World Showcase nation offers special hands-on activities as part of Kids Day Celebrations. Each celebration is different, but the theme is always the same: All kids, no matter where they live, like to have fun.

Past events include ribbon dancing in China, face painting in Canada, sidewalk chalk art in the United Kingdom, watercoloring in France, piñata decorating in Mexico, storytelling in Norway, script lessons in Morocco, "chicken dancing" in Germany, puppet shows in Italy, hula hoop contests in The American Adventure, and chopstick races in Japan. Check the entertainment schedule to see if a celebration is planned during your visit.

Disney-MGM Studios

Sorcery in the Sky Fireworks: During the summer and holiday seasons, you can see the World's most amazing fireworks, set to music from Hollywood's biggest films, including Disney's *Fantasia*. Check your entertainment schedule to see if it's happening during your visit.

Afternoon Parade: A brand-new parade is expected to come to the Studios. The theme will be the same as Disney's animated film *Toy Story*. It's all about the funny adventures of toys that come to life when humans are not around. Be sure to check your entertainment schedule for the exact time of the parade.

WONDERS OF THE WORLD

Kids ages 10 through 15 with a special interest in art, entertainment, international culture, or the environment can sign up for a six-hour backstage learning adventure. There are four programs to choose from. We got a special tour with a brief overview of two of them.

Art Magic: Bringing Illusion to Life shows how artists at Walt Disney World create the illusion of reality in movies and the theme parks. This adventure includes a behind-the-scenes look at the animation process. You get to paint your own animation cel. You also learn about the use of theme, color, and forced perspective. At the end of the day, you get a chance to draw your own Disney characters, using secret tips shared during your backstage adventure.

"If you really want to know how they make a cartoon or create animation, this is the place to go," says Justin. Dawna agrees. "I like the animation part the best," she says, "because you get to see all of the steps it takes to make a movie, and a hands-on chance to try it yourself."

Show Biz Magic: The Walt Disney World of Entertainment introduces you to the wide range of entertainment at Walt Disney World. You discover the importance of communication, show preparation, auditions, being a good audience, and star qualities. You learn first-hand by talking with performers. Highlights include a visit to the wig and makeup room located in a tunnel beneath the Magic Kingdom.

All the kids found something to like about this adventure. "I think land to land, talking with international cast members and learning about different types of architecture. You also find out how to communicate in other languages, decode ancient hieroglyphics, and uncover the secrets of world-famous landmarks.

Wildlife Adventure: Exploring the Environment takes you on a safari through the Walt Disney World conservation area. You take part in discussions on wildlife identification, ecosystems, and environmental issues. You also get to observe alligators, birds, snakes, and other creatures in their natural habitat.

everybody should go to this because it explains what goes on behind the scenes," says Tate. Lindsay thinks "it's exciting to see how they get the live characters ready with wigs and makeup." Adam says, "I love this program. It's really neat how we learned about the parade floats and how they work."

Passport: A Secret Mission to Other Lands brings to life the traditions, art, culture, and history of the countries in Epcot's World Showcase. You travel from

The cost is $79 for each program. It includes access to the theme parks and backstage areas during each program, lunch, and a personalized certificate of completion. For reservations, call 407-354-1855.

SHOPPING

It's easy to get overwhelmed by the number of shops at Walt Disney World. Shopping is an important part of your vacation, but you should decide in advance how much you can spend.

Most kids bring some of their own money. Dawna suggests saving up to buy souvenirs because "some things are really expensive." Whether you're spending your own money or your parents', be careful not to buy the first thing you see. You're bound to find something you like better later on. A good place to shop is the Disney Village Marketplace. "Everything you'd want is right there," says Dawna.

Here are some suggestions for souvenirs in several price ranges. Keep in mind that these prices are subject to change.

Under $5

Buttons	$ 1.50
Magnets	$ 2.75
Posters	$ 3.95
Mousketeer ears	$ 4.25
Pins	$ 4.95
Keychains	$ 4.95

Under $10

Wallets	$ 5.95
Sunglasses	$ 5.98
Character banks	$ 6.95
Minnie ears	$ 7.95
Waist pouches	$ 9.95

Under $20

Baseball caps	$10.95
WDW calendars	$10.95
Plush characters	$10.95
Simba hats	$12.95
Mickey gloves	$12.95
Hair accessories	$12.95
Plush hats	$14.95
Tote bags	$14.95
"M" baseball caps	$14.95
Clocks	$16.95
Backpacks	$18.95
Videos	$19.95

Under $25

Sweatshirts	$22.00
Plush characters	$22.95
Clocks	$24.00

Hot Tips

In this chapter, we'll give you advice on how to get the most out of your Walt Disney World trip. There are lots of planning suggestions, plus hints on making schedules, getting along with your parents, and many other tips the kids discovered on our trip. You may want to take notes as you go along since there's a lot to remember. There's also an explanation of the Disney lingo used in this book. So read on for some hot tips from the kids for the most awesome vacation in the World!

Turn the page for lots of hot tips!

GETTING READY TO GO

When to Go

Deciding when to visit Walt Disney World can be confusing. Karyn warns that "you can't do anything when it's really crowded." Nita says, "If you're not a person who likes crowds, go during the winter. In the summer the lines are long for everything." Brian agrees. "Definitely don't go during a holiday when school is out."

To avoid crowds, try to visit during the first two weeks in December. The weather is still nice, and you can see all the Christmas shows and decorations. If the only time you can visit is during a school vacation or in the

summer, allow plenty of extra time and plan your days carefully so you don't spend your entire vacation in line.

During less crowded times, especially in January, attractions may be closed for renovations. And if you want to go swimming, avoid January and February, when it's often too cool. Also, the water parks usually close for renovations for a few weeks during the winter months.

Making a Schedule

The kids agree that you should definitely make a schedule. Karyn says, "The schedule doesn't have to be that detailed, just planned out so you basically know what you want to do. I would use this guide to plan out the whole trip before leaving home." Anna agrees. "There's no way you'll get to see everything. This book will help you decide beforehand your 'must-sees.'"

Ashley suggests that "you read the guide and then sit down with your parents and see what everyone else wants to do." Nita agrees. "Work with your parents on the schedule, so you all get to do the things you want to do." Robert advises that "the book is your best tour guide because it tells you about all the rides. If it says the Haunted Mansion is scary and you don't like scary rides, then you know not to go on it."

First you should decide how many days to spend in each park. The kids agree that the ideal trip would last about ten days. They also agree that the minimum amount of time is about five days. You need at least two days for the Magic Kingdom, two days for Epcot, and a full day for the Disney-MGM Studios. Tate suggests, "Go to the Magic Kingdom first, then to the Disney-MGM Studios, and then to Epcot."

Write for more information: Walt Disney World Box 10,000 Lake Buena Vista, FL 32830

Karyn suggests "including a day of swimming and relaxing. Don't try to do everything at once, because if you're tired it's no fun." On hot days, it's a good idea to leave the parks, get your hand stamped, and go back to the hotel for lunch or a swim.

Plan each day by choosing the best time to see each attraction. To avoid the longest lines, follow the advice in the theme park tips that begin on page 152. Try to be flexible, and allow extra time in the schedule for surprises.

On the next page, there's some space for you to begin writing your family's schedule.

149

My Visit to Walt Disney World

Day 1

Day 2

Day 3

Day 4

Day 5

Packing Tips

When you pack, make sure you're prepared for either warm or cool weather. Layers are a good idea, so you can take something off if you get hot. You don't need dressy clothes. Shorts or jeans and T-shirts are fine for just about everywhere. Here's a list to get you started:

- This book.
- Activities to keep you busy on the plane or in the car—books, magazines, puzzles, or hand-held video games.
- A sweatshirt or sweater.
- Shorts and jeans.
- Long-sleeved and short-sleeved shirts.
- Bathing suits.
- Broken-in sneakers or shoes.
- Sunscreen and a hat.
- Camera and extra film.
- Backpack for your stuff.

My Packing List

" Be prepared for a lot of walking. "
—Robert (age 8)

MAGIC KINGDOM TIPS

• Get to the park early so you're at the end of Main Street when the rest of the park opens.

• Check the Tip Board at the end of Main Street. It tells you how long the wait is for the most popular attractions.

• You won't have to wait as long if you go to Space Mountain, Splash Mountain, Big Thunder Mountain, Pirates of the Caribbean, and Fantasyland either first thing in the morning or during the 3 P.M. Mickey Mania parade.

• Another great time to visit the top attractions is at night, during or after the SpectroMagic parade. You can usually get right on without waiting.

• If there are two lines, the one on the left is almost always shorter.

• Save time for souvenir shopping on Main Street.

• Never eat before riding Space Mountain, Splash Mountain, or Big Thunder Mountain Railroad.

• If you're looking for the park with the most rides for kids, head to the Magic Kingdom.

• Don't be afraid to go on Big Thunder Mountain Railroad unless you really hate roller coasters. Avoid Splash Mountain if you hate big drops.

• There are several "chicken exits" in the line for Space Mountain, so you can change your mind at the last minute.

If you want to see an attraction more than once, try it again after dark when lines are usually shorter.

152

EPCOT TIPS

- Start your day at the Wonders of Life pavilion, where you'll want to get on Body Wars and see Cranium Command first thing in the morning.
- At 11 A.M., head over to World Showcase (that's when it opens). Go back to Future World in the afternoon when it's less crowded.
- Check the Tip Board in Innoventions Plaza. It tells you how long the wait is for many attractions.
- Save time for all the interactive exhibits at Innoventions, Image Works, The Living Seas, and Wonders of Life.
- Don't miss the Leap Frog Fountains outside the Journey Into Imagination pavilion, where streams of water jump from fountain to fountain.
- Buy a passport at any World Showcase shop and get it stamped in every country. It's a great reminder of your trip.
- The best place to watch IllumiNations is from the little island between Italy and The American Adventure.
- Take a guided tour of the countries in World Showcase in the Wonders of the World program. See page 145 for details.
- Try not to see the movies at Canada, France, and China all in a row.
- Take time to talk to the people who work in World Showcase. They all come from the country of the pavilion they represent, and they have many interesting stories to tell.

DISNEY-MGM STUDIOS TIPS

- Arrive at the Disney-MGM Studios before the posted opening time. The gates usually open about a half-hour before the scheduled time.
- The character breakfast at the Soundstage restaurant is a great way to start the day.
- See Muppet*Vision 3-D, Voyage of the Little Mermaid, and Star Tours in the morning before the lines get too long.

- Tower of Terror has very long lines. See it early in the day and never right after a meal.
- There is one "chicken exit" at Tower of Terror, right before you get on the ride elevator, just in case you change your mind at the last minute.
- Some attractions don't open until late morning. Be sure to check your entertainment schedule for exact showtimes.
- Check the Studios Tip Board at the end of Hollywood Boulevard. It tells you which attractions are about to begin a new show, and which have the shortest lines.
- Get a good spot along Hollywood Boulevard to see the afternoon parade.
- Don't miss the newest attraction, The Spirit of Pocahontas Stage Show.

154

MORE TIPS

- Try to eat lunch early in the day. Then you can go on rides while everyone else is eating lunch and the lines will be shorter.
- Once you have seen the three theme parks, check out Discovery Island and the Wonders of the World programs.
- Bring rain ponchos or an umbrella because you never know when it will rain. You also can buy bright yellow Mickey ponchos all around Walt Disney World.
- Do your shopping at the Disney Village Marketplace.
- Bring gum if you like it, because it's not sold anywhere at Walt Disney World.

Where the Lines Are

Here's a list of rides that have long lines. Some are worth the wait, no matter how long. Others can be great fun, especially if you save them for a time when they're less crowded.

Rides Worth the Wait

Space Mountain
Splash Mountain
Big Thunder Mountain Railroad
The Twilight Zone Tower Of Terror
Legend Of The Lion King
Cranium Command
Body Wars
Jim Henson's Muppet*Vision 3-D
Star Tours
Pirates Of The Caribbean
The Magic Of Disney Animation

Save for Another Time

Country Bear Jamboree
Dumbo, The Flying Elephant
It's A Small World
Mad Tea Party
Skyway
Jungle Cruise
Spaceship Earth Show
Journey Into Imagination Ride
Voyage of the Little Mermaid
Honey, I Shrunk The Audience

TRAVELING WITH YOUR PARENTS
(and brothers and sisters)

If you follow our hints for working out a schedule with your parents and brothers and sisters before you go, it will be easier to include something for everyone.

Remember that your parents are looking forward to this vacation as much as you are. Lissy warns, "Don't try to force your parents to do things that will make them unhappy because they will act unhappy." But don't worry, as Nita says, "No matter how old you are, you'll always love Disney World."

Here are a few hints to help everyone get along:
● Go to the most popular attractions early in the day so you don't argue about waiting in long lines. To ride the best attractions a second time, wait and go during a parade or at night, when the rides are less crowded.
● Your parents will want to see the movies in World Showcase at Epcot. Plan your day so you begin at the Wonders of Life pavilion with Body Wars and Cranium Command. Later on head for the countries with the movies. Try not to see them all in a row. Remember, you have to stand for the movies in Canada and China. You get to sit down for the France movie. A good way to break up the movies is to go on the boat ride at Norway.
● Talk your parents into taking a break for ice cream or another snack in the late afternoon. Everyone gets tired of walking, so a cool drink or snack is refreshing.
● Have your entire family wear the same hat or shirt color so it's easy to stay together.

- The kids agree that Walt Disney World is more fun when you're there with other kids. Bring younger brothers and sisters (ages 2 to 7) to the Magic Kingdom. They'll really like Mickey's Starland; Dumbo, The Flying Elephant; It's A Small World; Cinderella's Golden Carrousel; and the Country Bear Jamboree. For kids who might be afraid of the dark, avoid Peter Pan's Flight, Snow White's Adventures, Pirates of the Caribbean, Mr. Toad's Wild Ride, and especially the Haunted Mansion and Alien Encounter. The kids also agree they'd like to play with younger siblings at the Honey, I Shrunk the Kids Movie Set Adventure playground at the Disney-MGM Studios.

- If you're an older kid, you might want to split up from your parents for a while. Agree on a meeting time and place, and be sure you don't get in any long lines too close to your set time. Don't meet at Cinderella Castle—it's too crowded.

- If you turn around and your parents have disappeared, or if they don't show up at your agreed-upon meeting place, you should go to Baby Services or City Hall in the Magic Kingdom, Guest Relations near Innoventions or Baby Services next to the Odyssey Center in Epcot, or Guest Relations near the front gate at the Disney-MGM Studios. Just ask a park employee and he or she will point you in the right direction.

"**Get a lot of rest, because if you're exhausted you can't do anything.**"

—Brian (age 12)

WHERE TO FIND THE CHARACTERS

Check the entertainment schedule for the theme park you're visiting so you can catch the character shows there throughout the day. Mickey and his friends visit all three parks, so you can say hello and maybe even take a picture with them. It's fun to get the characters' autographs either inside the back cover of this book or in a special autograph book. Here are some clues about where you might find them.

Magic Kingdom: There's a "Once Upon A Time" character breakfast in King Stephan's Banquet Hall every morning, where you can meet Cinderella and friends. At other times you might find her in the restaurant's lobby. More characters appear next to City Hall throughout the day. Everyone gets a turn to meet them and have a photo taken.

Fantasyland is a really good place to find characters. Stop by the Fantasyland Pavilion near Dumbo, the Flying Elephant, to see who's there. Rafiki, Timon, and Pumbaa often hang out in Fantasyland, too. The best place to meet Mickey is at Mickey's Starland, where he and his Disney Afternoon cartoon friends star in a show. You can get a picture with Mickey at the Hollywood Theatre.

Epcot: Character meals are held for breakfast, lunch, and dinner at the Garden Grill Restaurant. The characters stop at each table so you can get some great pictures. Also, the characters are often out in front of the pavilions in World Showcase, wearing costumes from the different countries. Mickey and his pals often drop by the garden near the back of the United Kingdom pavilion. Another great place to meet characters is the rose garden

Disney Lingo

Audio-Animatronics:
Lifelike figures, from birds and hippos to movie stars and presidents. They seem so real—even thogh they're not.

Buffeteria:
The Disney word for cafeteria.

Cel:
The actual painted film used in an animated movie.

Imagineer:
The Disney name for a creative engineer who designs theme park attractions.

beside The American Adventure pavilion. Here, there's a good chance you'll get to see Disney's newest character, Pocahontas.

Disney-MGM Studios: You can go to the character breakfast at the Soundstage Restaurant to meet Aladdin, Jasmine, and the Genie, or Pocahontas, John Smith, and Meeko. You might also see them hanging out on Sunset Boulevard. If you want to meet Mickey, don't look for him on Mickey Avenue. He's almost always over on Sunset Boulevard. There, you can get in line to pose for a picture with him.

So who's on Mickey Avenue? Lots of the other characters, like Belle and the Beast. Go in the afternoon when there aren't as many people, and you can get a ton of pictures.

TIPS FOR TAKING PICTURES

- In each park there are Photo Spots marked by little signs with cameras on them. Photos taken from these spots will turn out best.
- It's fun to bring your own disposable camera. These cameras are easy to use and carry, and you'll have your own pictures to paste in this book as a reminder of your trip.
- Bring lots of film.
- Make sure your fingers aren't in front of the lens.
- Don't shoot too close or too far away from your subject.
- You cannot take pictures inside the attractions.
- Your parents will probably take lots of pictures of you with the characters. It would be fun to take pictures of your parents with *their* favorite characters.

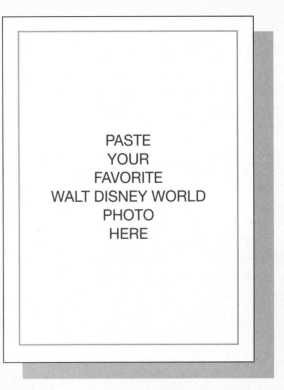

PASTE
YOUR
FAVORITE
WALT DISNEY WORLD
PHOTO
HERE